AF469382

# The Coca-Cola Art of
# JIM HARRISON

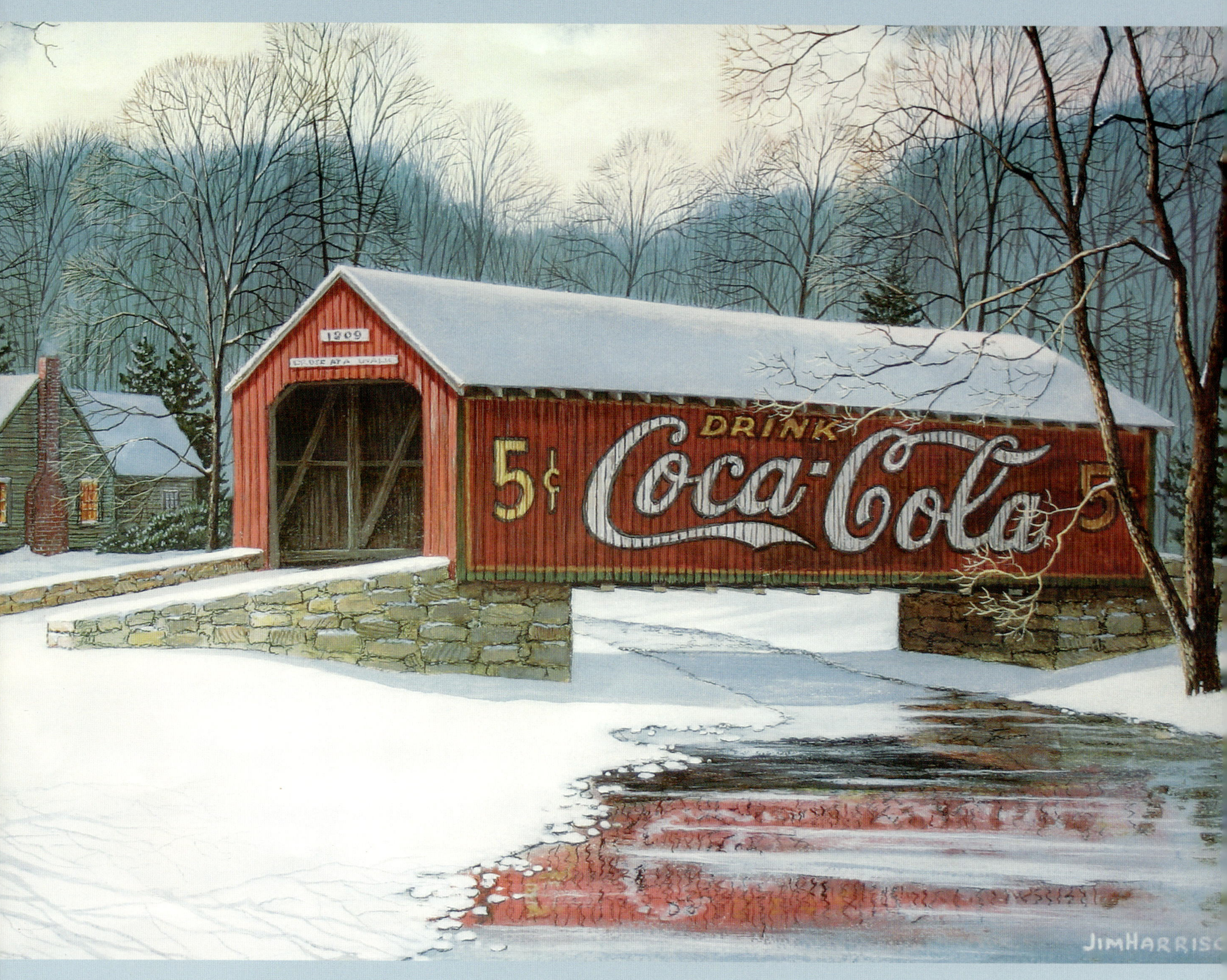
1909
DRINK
5¢
Coca-Cola

# The *Coca-Cola* Art of JIM HARRISON

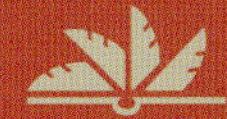

THE UNIVERSITY OF SOUTH CAROLINA PRESS

Special thanks go to Donald Brandt of Earhardt, South Carolina,
who owns many of Jim Harrison's Coca-Cola paintings
in a private family foundation collection.

Published by the University of South Carolina Press
Columbia, South Carolina 29208

www.sc.edu/uscpress

Manufactured in the China

26 25 24 23 22 21 20 19 18 17    10 9 8 7 6 5 4 3 2 1

*Library of Congress Cataloging-in-Publication Data*
Names: Harrison, Jim, 1936– artist.
The CocaCola art of Jim Harrison / Jim Harrison.
Columbia, South Carolina : The University of South Carolina Press, 2017. | Includes index.
LCCN 2016047773 (print) | LCCN 2016047982 (ebook) | ISBN 9781611177268
(hardcover : alk. paper) | ISBN 9781611177275 (ebook)
LCSH: Harrison, Jim, 1936– —Themes, motives. | Coca Cola (Trademark) in art. | Americana in art.
LCC ND237.H335 A4 2016 (print) | LCC ND237.H335 (ebook) | DDC 759.13—dc23
LC record available at https://lccn.loc.gov/2016047773

To J. J. Corn4th, sign painter, who took me under his wing early in my life when I needed him most. He was my only lifeline to the world of creativity. He taught me the art of hand lettering and show-card writing that has served me well for sixty-five years. Little did he or I know that our working on Coca-Cola signs would one day be such a big part of this book.

A special thank you to Deidre Mercer Martin, who is not only my right hand but also my left hand. She is a valued assistant who always does many things for me even before I know they need to be done. She is the workhorse and the wordsmith behind this book.

And to my wife, Margaret, who is with me every step of the way.

# • CONTENTS •

# ABOUT THE ARTIST

*Deidre Mercer Martin*

When young Jim Harrison climbed atop the scaffold in the summer of 1952 to paint his first Coca-Cola sign, little did he know that he was beginning a life-long love of the Coca-Cola trademark and launching a career as one of America's foremost landscape artists. From his early experiences, Jim developed a passion for preserving the past, especially rural America.

Jim was born in his grandmother's house in Leslie, Georgia, January 1936. When Jim was six years old, his father took a job with American Telephone and Telegraph Company in Denmark, South Carolina. Jim was quite involved in the activities of Denmark High School. As the "class artist," he was kept busy with the annual, school newspaper, and class bulletin boards. His first love was athletics, in which he excelled and was named all state in both football and basketball. During high school summer vacations, he worked as an assistant to a seventy-year-old sign painter, J. J. Cornforth. The elder gentleman taught the aspiring artist how to letter, and for several summers the two traveled the rural areas around Denmark, painting Coca-Cola bulletins on the sides of barns and country stores. After high school graduation, Jim entered the University of South Carolina.

Torn between his love of art and the enjoyment of athletics, he pursued a dual major in art and physical education. In 1960 he embarked on a successful eleven-year high school coaching career. But when the time came to choose, his passion for creating memorable works of art and preserving rural America was the stronger influence. In 1970 he declined an offer to join the Furman University football coaching staff and returned to his hometown of Denmark.

In 1972 Jim had no knowledge of the art market, but with enthusiasm he headed to New York City for the Fall Greenwich Village Sidewalk Show. His only sale during the three-week show was an 85-dollar original, and his expenses for the entire experience came to 800 dollars. Several years on the sidewalk circuit served him well as he learned his trade and the business of art. After several years Jim had ten galleries selling his originals. He published his first limited-edition print, *Coastal Dunes,* in 1973 gaining the attention of the nation's leading publisher of limited-edition art prints, Frame House Gallery of Louisville, Kentucky.

This partnership with Frame House Gallery helped establish Jim as a leader of a major twentieth-century art movement, "Art for Everyone." Jim had the right idea, the right subject matter, and the right partner, Wood Hannah, who owned Frame House Gallery Publishers. All of it together put Jim at the right place at the right time. Neither Hannah nor the artist realized the far-reaching impact that their new limited-edition concept was beginning to have on the rural South and ultimately the whole art world. Jim's desire to make his work available to everyone matched Hannah's goal of reaching even the smallest rural communities. The mutual goals led to high quality promotional art prints that Hannah required the dealers to buy and give away during artist appearances. Jim made personal appearances all over the United States and autographed thousands of the free prints. The majority of the participating public was in direct contact with a real-life artist and an art gallery for the first time. The average rural southerner at the time was intimidated by the thought of visiting an art museum and had a very limited connection to art and artists. Jim's efforts and successes served as a model for many other aspiring artists to find their way to full-time status.

As Jim's success as an artist grew, Coca-Cola remained dear to his heart, and he became an avid collector of old Coca-Cola signs. His studio is lined with a vast array of this collection, many of which have served as inspirations in his paintings. In 1975 he painted a country store that still had visible one of the old faded signs Cornforth and Jim had painted 20 years earlier. The painting was put into print, and *Disappearing America* was released as a limited-edition print at 40 dollars by Frame House Gallery. It became an immediate success, selling out all 1,500 prints in the edition. This was one of first Coca-Cola collector prints ever put on the market, projecting Jim on the national scene through the publisher's network of 400 dealers. He became the undisputed nation's leader in rural Americana art, with this print and many of his prints appreciating up to 3,000 percent of their original value.

Since entering into a licensee relationship with Coca-Cola in 1995, he has continued developing limited-edition prints featuring the trademark. His annual Coca-Cola Calendar is a popular collector's item with sales across the country. He has been a licensee of the Coca-Cola Company for more than 20 years. This relationship is a visible demonstration of his love of the well-known trademark, which he first painted on the side of an old barn while a 14-year-old apprentice of the elderly sign painter J. J. Cornforth.

Jim's success is now evidenced by his nearly 50 years as a full-time artist. Turning his back on the more familiar path—a career in high school and college athletics—he embraced his dream to become an artist. With talent, hard work and perseverance, he has more than 100 sold-out limited editions of prints made from his paintings and is followed by thousands of collectors of his work across the country. He has also had successful one-man shows at the prestigious Hammer Galleries in New York City and the Conacher Gallery in San Francisco, and the annual shows at the prestigious National Academy Gallery in New York have included his paintings.

In addition to his artwork, Jim is the author or illustrator of several books including *The Palmetto Tree and Its South Carolina Home, Pathway to a Southern Coast, Country Stores, American Christmas, The Passing, Jim Harrison Cookbook: Southern Cooking and Southern Stories,* and *Jim Harrison: His World Remembered.*

In 2008 Jim was honored by Governor Mark Sanford of South Carolina with the prestigious Order of the Palmetto Award for his many years of service as a citizen of our state and was honored for his many contributions to art and the State of South Carolina by the South Carolina House of Representatives. Citing him as a "nationally and internationally acclaimed artist" and as "one of the Palmetto State's Chief Art Treasures," the resolution congratulated Jim on his many years as a successful artist and on the occasion of the 20th anniversary of Jim Harrison Gallery in Denmark, S.C. In May 2010 he was awarded an honorary Doctorate of Fine Arts by the University of South Carolina for his many successful years as a professional artist, the prestige he has brought to the university and the state, and his generosity to a wide range of charitable organizations. In 2014 the South Carolina General Assembly named the main intersection in Denmark, South Carolina, as "Harrison Crossroads" in his honor with a joint resolution declaring that it was "fitting and proper to recognize one of this nation's premier artists by naming the intersection that borders his art gallery in his honor." •

*During the process of publishing this book, Jim passed away on June 18, 2016. He will be remembered through his work as a great South Carolinian and an American treasure. As Jim says in this book, his art career began with Coca-Cola—so this book seems fitting in many ways as a lasting reminder of his lifelong love affair with this American icon.*

# My Coca-Cola Story

## Denmark Was a Coca-Cola Town

My little community, Denmark, South Carolina, was a Coca-Cola® town. You better believe it, and Clifford Ray, the owner of the Denmark Coca-Cola Bottling Company, made certain of it. He did everything in his power to be sure that the famous iconic trademark was the only soft-drink advertisement showing on our storefronts. The red or white Spenserian script logo was recognizable to everyone—even by those who could not read. He wanted everyone to be aware of the pleasure of drinking an ice-cold Coca-Cola in a bottle or enjoying a soda-fountain version from either of the local drug stores.

The Ray family obviously had a very profitable monopoly, but we knew they were willing to give back to the community and to those who supported the product. Even as early as when we were in the third grade, Mr. Ray began making his impression on us. I well remember Septembers, when he would come to the elementary school, dressed in a white-and-green striped Coca-Cola uniform. He would speak briefly about Coke® and give each student a Coca-Cola writing tablet and a red pencil. The teacher was presented with a new wall clock and a calendar. Later that day at recess, we were all served cookies and cold Coca-Cola from an ice cooler in the back of a yellow Coca-Cola truck. Unofficially this was Coca-Cola Day in the Denmark schools.

At that time, 70 years ago, local Coca-Cola bottlers furnished the schools professionally printed athletic schedules that were posted in storefront windows all over town. Large porcelain signs praising the teams and also including their schedules were erected in some visible downtown areas. The scoreboard for every high school sport bore the scripted Coca-Cola logo. Coca-Cola was a part of our lives, and there were reminders that nudged us from every direction.

The Denmark bottler controlled the soft-drink business in the area, and he was rewarded by customer loyalty. Concession stands on movable trailers were furnished by him for any local event. The trailers were covered with a yellow awning and red-and-white Coca-Cola signs. He left no opportunities for other competing soft drinks. He was simply following the lead of the parent company, which itself poured money into the continuous promotion of the sweet drink of Atlanta, Georgia, and expected the local bottlers to do likewise.

Myself and others of my age certainly have varied, lifelong, and fond memories of our annual visits to the bottling room at the Coca-Cola plant. The whole operation was visible at all times from outside, but we were allowed inside. We were fascinated, watching as the bottles by the hundreds were filled individually and capped automatically on a moving conveyer belt right before our eyes. Each field trip to the plant netted us another serving of Coke and a small hat with the Coca-Cola logo. Mr. Ray was certainly an aggressive but very nice ambassador for the drink, and his sweet treats earned our respect and loyalty.

And so somewhere in this true story was born the strong lifetime love affair between Jim Harrison the artist and Coca-Cola. My interest went further, deeper, and in a different direction than that of my schoolmates. My attention was fully captivated as I watched our local sign painter, J. J. Cornforth, hand paint the large Coca-Cola bulletins on the fronts and the sides of the stores. Several days of scraping and background preparation preceded the actual painting, which was a sight for this young aspiring painter to watch and dream about.

J. J. Cornforth had a degree of celebrity status as he seemed to have an apparent gift or talent allowed only to the select few. I kept my distance, but every chance that I got I watched in awe, and I felt that what he was doing I could learn to do—with time and practice. His finished Coca-Cola wall bulletins became art masterpieces in my thinking, and I began to form a goal in the back of my mind. J. J. Cornforth was my first live connection to the world of art, and Coca-Cola was to become my first serious subject matter.

## Working for J. J. Cornforth

In early summer in 1952, I walked in the door of J. J. Cornforth's Signs and inquired about a summer job. More than 60 years later, I walk in the same door every day to my own gallery to work on fine-art paintings. Today I work at a homemade easel very similar to the sign painter's version that Mr. Cornforth had in his sign shop. So much has changed in half a century, and yet so much is still the same. Mr. Cornforth is gone, but the lessons and skills I learned from that old gentleman have certainly served me well through the years.

I still use the very same mahl stick that he made for me half a century ago. Such a stick is a standard must-have for lettering signs and is necessary to steady the painting hand and assist in manipulating fine quill lettering brushes. Current versions are made of aluminum and can be folded for easier packing in artist and sign painter kits. Mr. Cornforth made ours using standard one-yard-long ⅜-inch wooden dowels, and he glued 1½-inch fishing corks on the end. I have some of the more recent store-bought models, but to this day I always find myself using the old sidekick made for me in the 1950s.

The corked end was placed against the sign background, and the other end was held with the left hand, allowing the painting hand to rest and be steadied on the stick. I now rely on the stick for steadiness in making precise detailed strokes on original canvas paintings. After over five decades of continuous use, mine is now covered with stains and niches from much wear and tear. We used sanding paper to keep the cork clean and occasionally sanded the dowel of any drops of paint or splinters. My old stick is very smooth from much handling and use, and I continue to keep it sanded and ready for use even in its worn condition.

I paint with acrylics thinned with water so there is no odor, but the old scents of Mr. Cornforth's sign shop are still very familiar to me. I love the smell of oil paint, turpentine, thinner, and chalk dust, and a whiff of it anywhere rushes my mind back to those early sign shop days.

I didn't immediately start lettering signs, but my education began that very first day. Neatness was the order of every day and every job. "We paint signs, and we don't paint ourselves" was hounded into me by my teacher. Mr. Cornforth never had paint stains on his clothes or hands. It was and still is my nature to work neatly, and very rarely do I get unintended paint on anything.

"Work with your right protected" was another rule. We wanted nothing to bump our hand or paint container as we worked so the paint was placed to our right and protected from being knocked over. I continue to insist that my worktables have small elevated edges so nothing slips off. I work with my artist palette in front of me, but the rules of care and caution are still ingrained in my thinking. I don't have paint stains on my clothes, and any paint that gets on my hands, the table, or the floor is immediately wiped very clean and dry.

Yes, Mr. Cornforth was my first art teacher, my mentor, and my friend. He was full of information and wisdom that I sought at every chance. He took an immediate liking to me and referred to me as his young, gifted apprentice. I knew nothing of the real meaning of apprenticeship arrangements but later realized that most sign painter's helpers aspired and worked toward learning the skill that would become their vocation for life.

Life didn't mean anything to me then, as my life was lived from day to day and from one athletic season to the next. But that first summer day turned into that whole summer and the next few summers. In those days, as I continue to do today, I wake up every morning excited about getting to work.

I was assigned all scraping jobs and training me how to block in the backgrounds was managed very quickly. The big wall Coca-Cola bulletins were not repainted every year so for that I had to wait. I was immediately given the responsibility of cleaning and refreshing the porcelain Coca-Cola privilege signs, but Mr. Cornforth made the pounce patterns, and he did the lettering.

The custom pounce patterns were made on a 4' by 8' tilted table similar to a store-bought drawing or drafting table, but ours was homemade and unusually large. We could tilt it to suit our preferences and job. A long T square, also homemade, would slide along the bottom of the table to make the standard 90-degree mark for straight-sided letters. "Make a good straight-sided 'I,' and you can make half the alphabet and half of the other half of the alphabet. Do it straight, Jimmy." I heard this over and over. Sensing my eagerness to learn, Mr. Cornforth offered to meet with me at his shop after hours to help with my lettering. I was not to be paid for those hours, but I immediately took him up on the offer. Several of the first nights were spent learning how to hold a quill or greyhound brush with no paint on them. Actual strokes were simulated on cardboard to learn the feel of turning and twisting. "No! Keep it straight, keep it parallel, Jimmy. Keep it straight, vertical, and parallel" was sternly said many times.

First I was to learn to perfectly make the capital letter "I" about 12 inches tall and 2 inches wide. Later I learned that determining the width was dictated by the total available sign background space. Spacing was difficult and perfected only by many hours of practice yet aided by some natural taste for what looked right.

Today's computer-driven mechanical spacing will never have the artistic look of a professionally hand-lettered sign of years ago. What now is produced in a few minutes with a keyboard and the touch of a mouse took us hours back then.

And so it was that I was fascinated by my summertime job and the challenge of being only the second person in my little town who could letter signs. Sign painters in that time were recognized for their unique skills, and they seemed always to intrigue observers.

In that first summer I probably grew more professionally than during any other period of time in my life. I scraped away flaking paint and repainted brick and wooden walls with white to block out existing paint by day, but my young ego was rewarded by night with several hours of tedious instruction from my elderly master.

With an overload of determination and aspiration I would follow my instruction sessions with more hours of practice on my drawing table, which my father made for me in my upstairs attic bedroom. With a red sable postcard brush and a jar of black poster paint, I spent time well into the late night hours practicing making straight lines down the columns of newspaper print, twisting the brush slightly as I neared the top and the bottom so that a short horizontal stroke could neatly square off the ends of the straight letters.

The more difficult yet faster "flood" stroke was to come later. "Straighter, straighter, neater, neater"—these words were shouted at me with an encouraging tone that drove my young determined spirit to work more and get it right. And that I did in that wonderful summer of 1952. I learned to make two vertical lines with a connection in the middle forming an *H,* and then a *T,* and *F* and *E*. Slight variations formed *V*'s, *W*'s, and *N* and *M's*. Soon I could paint *HAT, MAT,* AND *THAT* very professionally.

Curved letters were not easy, but straight line accomplishments added the necessary confidence of stroke so necessary in sign painting. "Twist it Jimmy and keep it symmetrical" became the assigned nighttime lesson. The curved letters were more difficult to accomplish, but I knew that I was near the end of the lessons in basic letter forming. I dove in first with a *D* and then a *P*. The letter *C* was a little harder, but it was the *O* and the *S* that were the toughest. A sign painter eventually develops a knowledge or sense of how the letter should look. This comes only from study and practice.

I was a true student of the skill, and I sought all the information I could find. I subscribed to *Signs of the Times* magazine and from this publication I ordered several books that I read over and over. I couldn't get enough of the challenges of the trade. I wanted to be a sign painter just like Mr. Cornforth. I was determined. I really worked hard at it.

### My First Sign Job

I shall never forget the morning in early August of that first summer when I walked in the shop and on my easel was an eight-foot-wide white board already pounced with the outline for the words "Just Ahead." There were several dozen similar boards stacked nearby. Mr. Cornforth said "OK, Jimmy. I need those done today. Use that dark green that I mixed." This was the first time he actually gave me a job that required the lettering skills that I had learned. It was my first professional lettering job.

The pounce pattern outline that Mr. Cornforth had made kept me in place, but neatness and precision was my responsibility. Yes, a full day's worth of work on behalf of Mr. Cornforth, but a heaping load of pride was mine for the keeping. A pride in the job that kept growing as later I watched the Glass House Restaurant crew place those apron boards on the bottoms of their Highway 301 signs. I was excited, and I drove my mother, my father, and my girlfriend up and down Highway 301, just looking at my signs.

Other jobs followed, and my lettering skills and speed improved. Mr. Cornforth had developed a job ticket form that described the work to be done with a sketchy drawing of the sign layout and color notes. For larger signs we made full-size pounce patterns on the drawing table. As my ability improved, my dreams got bigger. I was eager for the anointment of confidence that all apprentices yearn to reach. Also the payoff time for the shopowner occurs when he can turn jobs over to his trained apprentice helper.

### The Restaurant Marquee

A late summer work order was placed in my box for the next day's work. "Jimmy, I want you to take care of the restaurant marquee by yourself tomorrow. You will need the eight-foot ladder, the pounce pattern, a one-inch fitch, and a three-inch cutter. Take the medium red gloss and a gallon of the gloss black. I'll probably stay in the shop." This was my first outside assignment alone, and it was on Main Street in Denmark. In the early morning I assembled my equipment and hurried off to the next block, where the very small Dew Drop Inn restaurant was located.

The pounce pattern fit exactly the sign space and left room at each end for two porcelain Coca-Cola round buttons that the bottler would have attached after the sign was dry. With no wind blowing, it was a fairly easy job to tape the pattern and pounce it heavy so as to show up on the freshly painted white background that I had prepared several days earlier. As I pounced from left to right and I got to the lower right end, I pounced in small letters the signature line "J. J. Corn4th Signs." In smaller letters under it Mr. Cornforth had pounced Jimmy Harrison. The Dew Drop Inn was my first signature job.

This was a "cut in" job where I painted the background around the letters leaving the letter space white. First there was to be a half-inch medium-red border that followed the pounce pattern and then a black background cut in on the outside of the red outline. Using a strong bristle fitch, I could keep the edges sharp and straight. Mortar joints varied in width but still they served as good vertical and horizontal guides. Spacing had already been determined in the making of the pounce pattern.

It was a full day's job for me with some drugstore breaks and going home for lunch. Mr. Cornforth walked down midafternoon, looked at the sign and said nothing but nodded to me, giving his approval. He then had a long cup of coffee inside with the owner before returning to the shop without a word of correction or criticism to me. No words from him were needed for me to know the pride he felt in having taught me. We never spoke of it.

### Back to School

Football practice started in mid-August, and the back-to-school mode set in. I assured Mr. Cornforth that I would work with him every weekend, school holidays, and again the next summer. I retained my excitement for my newly found ambition of sign painting, and I was committed to Mr. Cornforth.

My lettering skills became known to the teachers rather quickly, and I soon was the "go to" guy at school when small bulletin-board projects required lettering. I also began painting "Denmark Danes" on any vacant walls or doors that could be found, as well as on the blue athletic bus. The school principal gave me a spot in a vacant storage room for a supply cabinet and a small worktable. It jokingly became known as "Jimmy's Office." I had a key and a book satchel full of confidence, ambition, and pride.

I worked on the art for the school paper and the yearbook, and I painted the Dane on the gym floor. Requests for help with signs, bulletin boards, stage scenery and the junior-senior prom decorations afforded me time out of class and opportunities to further my "art career." However, athletics continued to be my first love, and never did I let anything interfere with that. My Saturdays were still spent assisting Mr. Cornforth, and I began tapering off my newspaper delivery job in the early mornings.

Thanksgiving and Christmas holidays were filled with sign-painting jobs at Mr. Cornforth's shop. I was being warned by my employer and mentor that the coming spring Saturdays and all summer would be filled with Coca-Cola work in that there were outdoor wall bulletins scheduled for repainting. I was excited as we viewed the new designs in the oversized painter's manuals furnished to us by the Coca-Cola Company. The new designs included images of bottles, bottle caps, and a variety of other choices that had to be worked out so they would fit the available wall spaces that Mr. Ray would acquire with agreements he would make with store owners.

Some agreements included painting the entire outside of the building in exchange for permission to put Coca-Cola signs in appropriate places. In such arrangements Mr. Ray got assurances that his drinks would have center stage promotions in the stores. Rivals, such Royal Crown and Pepsi, were around but not nearly as visible as Coke.

In early spring, decisions were made by Mr. Ray as to where the signs would go. Measuring and layout determinations were our responsibility, and we spent a number of the spring Saturdays on those decisions. Precise measurements were taken by us, and small-scale drawings for each location were prepared by Mr. Cornforth for Coca-Cola's approval. Once approved, we would receive full-size pounce patterns for each sign. Picture images would be a paint-by-the-numbers arrangement with color swatches and exact mixtures for the variety of colors. There was no other blending to be done as the large finished product was so well designed in Atlanta that it gave the desired look. I looked forward to the coming summer months, and, as soon as our baseball season was over, I started working afternoons with Mr. Cornforth.

The early summer heat made the wall preparations laborious and exhausting. The muscle part of the job was left to me and oftentimes a helper whom we would hire for the part-time work. Beginning early in the morning, we could escape the heat of the day. Several days of background preparation made the large walls ready for the signs. We would usually prepare two or three at a time and follow that with the finished sign in the next week or so. To average one completed sign a week was good as there was other work to be done in the shop. Truck lettering and school-bus lettering was always pressing Mr. Cornforth in the summer.

We maintained about 25 Coca-Cola bulletins that were 12 by 24 feet and larger. We had signs in Denmark and 15 miles beyond, including adjacent towns and locations at crossroads country stores. I enjoyed every minute of my job. It was at the crossroads stores that I learned to eat bologna and slab cheese on a raisin cinnamon roll as a sandwich. This seemed to be a sign painter's choice for on-the-job lunches. Our outside summer work occasionally matched us with other sign painters who were traveling for other companies affixing metal tack-ons or roof paintings. To hear these old wall dogs talk of earlier days traveling the country, painting signs, was like music to my ears. I envisioned it as a life of travel and excitement. Little did I realize that years later I would find that same excitement in my travels as I researched and sketched buildings such as the ones we were painting.

My second summer with Mr. Cornforth solidified my long-term connection to the Coca-Cola trademark. I began collecting little things with the logo on them, and Mr. Ray gave me a green-and-white jacket with Coca-Cola on the front and back. I wore it regularly.

The next school year found me pressured with more time required for school activities and yet a tiring Mr. Cornforth needing more of my time as well. I'm sure Mr. Cornforth thought I would take over his shop after my high school days, but my maturing thoughts did not include seeing myself in this as a career. He and I did agree that I would help as much as I could during my college days at the University of South Carolina, but he was trying to get away from the work. In time he retired, and I inherited the Coca-Cola work which I could handle during my summers off. I had my own little shop and bought an old cargo van with a place for my ladders on the top.

I seemed destined to remain connected with Coca-Cola, though, as it had worked out for me to continue the work during the summer months when I was teaching and coaching.

### Coach and Sign Man to Artist

For some years I was the Coca-Cola sign man for the Denmark Coca-Cola Bottling Company. While I began my coaching career in 1960, after graduating from the University of South Carolina, it just seemed to line up so that I had the right time off from my coaching job to maintain the wall bulletins in our area. Technology was beginning to nudge out the sign painter, and the Coca-Cola signs were becoming mass-produced items.

Things were changing, and the bottlers were gradually phasing out the painting of the walls by either giving up the locations or installing factory-printed metal signs. The storefront porcelain privilege signs were giving way to lighted plastic signs. The merchants names were put on the plastic panels by the manufacturers or decals were used by the local bottler. The sign man was becoming less and less needed. For me this was quite OK as my long-term ambitions were not solidly defined, and I didn't have a clear picture of how I wanted to live the rest of my life.

I floundered around several summers as partly sign painter, partly artist wanting to paint pictures. I was fully aware that I did not have the necessary skills to paint quality paintings, and I had no idea of how one made a living as an artist. Somewhere in those uncertain years, I learned of an art teacher, Miss Zeta Mellon, in Allendale. I was told some very good things about her, including that she had spent her career teaching art in and around New York. I longed for some connection to the New York art community, and I had never spoken to anyone that knew anything about it. Excitedly I made an early morning appointment with her, and that led to a major bonding that lasted for the rest of her life.

Miss Mellon had a special interest in me, and she took me under her wing. I looked forward to each day, arriving in her studio sometimes before she got up. I wanted her instruction, but equally important I had the opportunity to hear her stories of having spent summers in Woodstock, painting with some of the best artists in the country. She described the sidewalk shows in Greenwich Village with a romantic twist, and her knowledge of the galleries on 57th Street strengthened my resolve to find a way to be a part of the New York art scene.

The problem of participating in New York while not getting too far from Denmark loomed ahead, but I was to deal with that later. My first summer with her led to several more summers as I learned everything I could. But each summer, as the football season approached, I spent some days wishing summer would not end, and yet a few days of the smell of football equipment and the grassy field turned me back to my strong love of athletics. I had a hard time picturing myself not involved in coaching. I had not yet fulfilled one of my goals of being a head high school football coach. The chance to do so came in 1969, when Elloree High School came calling and offered me the position I desired. I threw myself into that season, but a chance at a full-time art career still loomed ahead and was always in the back of my mind.

As a good school year at Elloree High was coming to an end, my conflict between art and athletics was about to come to a head on collision. An unexpected offer to join the Furman University football staff, one that I had never dreamed of happening for me, had a bright glow to it. This was the opportunity of a lifetime and the dream of every high school coach. It was a difficult decision, but the tug of my love for Denmark and my love of art tilted my thinking in the other direction.

So it was in that spring of 1970 that I refused a college-coaching offer and resigned from my secure position as athletic director and head football coach at Elloree High School to become a full-time artist. I had instantly become unemployed with no income except what I could generate from producing and selling my art. I had previously sold a few paintings to friends, and I had several short Christmas vacation flings at being an artist in the local malls and on the sidewalk. Now this was serious do-or-die business.

## The Sidewalk Years

In 1972 I was aware of the upcoming Fall Greenwich Village Sidewalk Show in New York, and I decided that would be my starting place. I reasoned that, if I could be part of the New York art scene, I would have arrived and stated my professionalism. At least I would find out how to participate in that environment of sidewalk art shows and learn something about the business of art. I did learn, and learn well, from the Greenwich Village experience. There were many artists working and dreaming the same dreams. I already knew that I wanted more than the sidewalk circuit, but I was unsure of my goals and the way to reach them.

My wife, Margaret, and I were at the New York show for three weekends. On the Thursday night before the last weekend, we went up to 57th Street, where many of the famous commercial art galleries were located. After dinner we walked along 57th Street and happened upon Hammer Galleries, which was displaying an Eric Sloane barn painting in the front window.

I was stunned. This was it. I told Margaret this was where we wanted to be. This was our goal, and I knew then that one day I would have my painting in that window. Fifty-seventh Street was a big step up from down on the sidewalks in the Village, but we had a vision, a firm goal, and direction.

The third weekend of the sidewalk show brought my first sale as a full-time professional, and it was in New York. A very nice banker from Brooklyn walked up to my display and said he and his wife had to have my painting of a tobacco barn. He paid me the price of 85 dollars and left quite happy. I was excited and hurried to a telephone and called first my mama and then my teacher, Miss Mellon.

The total tally after Greenwich Village was that I had spent 800 dollars to be at the show and had taken in only the one sale for 85 dollars. Financially this was certainly not on the positive side; however, the experience was probably the best education that I could get for selling art. I made it a point to learn as much as I could from as many of the artists as possible. I learned about the "Sidewalk Circuit" as it was called and that there were opportunities every weekend if I were willing to travel. Most of the full-time artists who relied on sidewalk sales were geared up for a vagabond lifestyle. I did not see myself living that way long term and only thought of the sidewalk shows as a means to an end.

I returned home, having lived the experience of a lifetime. The perceived life of a sidewalk artist in New York had had such a romantic appeal to me for years, and I had always hoped to one day be a part of it. My close connection and affection for my hometown would never have allowed me to move away for any long periods, so learning of the sidewalk circuit and the many sidewalk opportunities around the country provided me a short-term business plan. I never envisioned myself a nomad who stayed on the road, following the shows from weekend to weekend, but rather I would travel to and from the shows—driving at night and allowing myself time at home during the week to paint and prepare for the weekend trips. I did this regularly for several years. I would paint Monday through Wednesday, pack up Thursday, and drive to that weekend's show and return on Sunday.

### The First Coca-Cola Painting

One week I had everything ready and packed for the weekend show, and I was just playing around at the easel. I took a 10" by 20" canvas and painted the background red. I cut around the trademark Coca-Cola leaving it white as I had done many times on much larger wall bulletins. I filled in the white letters and finished it off with a black outline and shadow around the letters. It was nothing more than just the Coca-Cola trademark against a red background on the canvas. Liking it and thinking it was "cool," I did two more in similar sizes and framed all three with our silver-and-black floater molding. I stuck them in one of the packing boxes with 45 dollars priced on the back of each one.

Set up time at the Orlando show started early in the morning of the first day, and often some serious buyers walked around during that time, hoping to get first choice on something they liked. The first shopper to come by our spot quickly bought one of the Coca-Cola paintings, and that was the beginning of 40-plus years of Jim Harrison Coca-Cola fine art. The second and third paintings also sold that first day. This was in the early seventies, and there was not the Coca-Cola memorabilia craze as we know it now. I knew immediately I was on to something, and I couldn't wait to get back to Denmark and fool around with some more Coca-Cola paintings.

The next week I did several similar paintings and four more with some variety of yellow or green borders adding the word *drink.* Amazingly the six new paintings brought us six new buyers at the next show. In the following weeks new wrinkles and some variety was added to more Coca-Cola paintings. The canvas was painted so as to resemble country-store wood siding, both horizontal and vertical. One weird canvas was square so I painted only the first few letters of the trade mark. Larger canvases and increased prices did not seem to slow down the selling. I was excited, and I began in earnest to research the designs of the earlier Coca-Cola signs. Although I experimented with other trademarks in a similar fashion and did get favorable responses to the different product names, nothing matched the success of the popular Coca-Cola trademark.

### The End of Sidewalk Days

At this point I had built relationships with a dozen or so art galleries who were selling my work. Tired of the constant preparation for sidewalk shows, I had become aware of limited-editions art prints and a company in Louisville, Kentucky, that was the leader in producing and selling them. I was fascinated and challenged by the thought of taking as much time as I needed to paint the very best painting that I could and have it turned into multiples by the limited-edition concept.

Then Margaret and I headed to the Virginia Beach show, which was successful, as we sold everything that we had and returned home with several thousand dollars profit. I reasoned that now I was going to clear my schedule and paint the very best coastal painting I could paint. I took a month and painted *Coastal Dunes* in 1973. It was nice, and, after showing it around to some frame shops, I was convinced that we should make prints.

I had Litho Krome Printers in Columbus, Georgia, produce 1,500 prints, which I signed and numbered 1 through 1,500. My established galleries began taking some of them, and sales increased rather quickly. Other frame shops sought me out and became our representatives in their particular areas. In time I had completed a complement to *Coastal Dunes,* which I named *Coastal Marshes,* and the 1,500 prints of this were also well received. I was excited about our success, but I realized that the larger publisher, Frame House Gallery with their 400-plus dealers all over the country, was a much better opportunity than what I could do by myself.

A direct approach one Sunday afternoon by telephone to the owner, Wood Hannah, got me an appointment the following day. I drove all night so as to be in Louisville the next morning. An immediate bond between Mr. Hannah and me resulted, and this turned out to be one of the best moves I made in my art career. I pitched to him the idea of a series of vanishing scenes of barns and country stores with old faded advertisements on them. He sensed the appeal these might have, and my career in advertising art was solidified that day in his office in Kentucky. My work was to immediately be thrust out to his dealers all across the country.

My goal was to paint a history of all the old advertisements and become the nation's leading advertising artist. *Mail Pouch Tobacco* was first, and it sold fairly well on release. Coca-Cola was next, and all 1,500 *Disappearing America* prints that were produced in 1975 sold out before it was released. That began 15 years of sold-out prints, with a new print released every three months. I became the advertising artist and painted many of the major trademarks, but I refused to repeat the Coca-Cola trademark. *Disappearing America* became my trademark piece, and the secondary market value soared from a release price of 40 dollars to more than 3,800 dollars.

Things were going very well for me and my art. I longed to return to New York, but especially to 57th Street and Hammer Galleries. It had become my backburner goal from the night that Margaret and I had looked in the window during the Greenwich Village Sidewalk Show.

A trip to New York and a meeting with Dick Lynch resulted in a long-term relationship with Hammer Galleries and four one-man shows. The first show featured the original of *Disappearing America,* and I had my chance to see it displayed in the very window where I first saw Eric Sloan's work years earlier. Little did I know it at that time, but Coca-Cola would become such a primary focus of my work for years to come.

### The Coca-Cola Art Years

It is difficult to pin point an exact starting time of Jim Harrison Coca-Cola art—such a journey there has been from 1952, during the days of J. J. Cornforth's sign shop, and then through the many years and experiences that have followed. There were smatterings of Coca-Cola fine art during the sidewalk years, but it was the Frame House Gallery connection that gave my art national exposure through the network of dealers all over the country. In hindsight the magic moment for Harrison Coca-Cola art was the release of *Disappearing America* as a fine-art limited-edition print by Frame House Gallery in 1975.

This was the first of many Harrison Coca-Cola fine-art prints and collectibles. The print was an instant success and remains our most sought-after collector print in our secondary market today. The 1975 release is considered to be one of the first Coca-Cola Collector prints published by anyone, and no other has reached its popularity. This all began at a time when Coca-Cola collectibles were not yet as popular as in more recent years.

The demand for *Disappearing America* prompted Frame House Gallery to want another Coca-Cola image immediately. I resisted the temptation and pressure, thinking that I needed to protect and enhance the collector value that was developing. I maintained that position for years, but much later I did decide to produce a poster for my Hammer Gallery show in New York and selected *Nickel Coca-Cola* for the image. It was released as a signed edition, and hundreds were sold immediately. I continue to reprint that image today, and it remains very popular.

Through the years I have visited the company archives, researching the records for earlier examples of outdoor signs. I have known many on staff, and they always seemed interested in what I was doing with my research and art. When *Disappearing America* was released, it was well received; many employees of the Coca-Cola Company purchased it as well. During this time I became more aware of the growing interest and market for Coca-Cola collectibles that had been developing. The Coca-Cola Collector Club was increasing in terms of number of members and activity. People were buying and wearing all sorts of items with the logo on them including caps, shirts, and belts.

For years I had a vast accumulation of old signs, coolers, vending machines, and other collectibles all around me. These things were becoming more sought after and much harder to find. I could begin to see more opportunity for my art, and it was clear to me that I needed to educate myself better as to what was going on in the marketplace.

In a short while, I was approached by a licensee, Trademark Marketing, and asked to produce a covered bridge painting with a Coca-Cola sign on it for their use. They wanted to manufacture metal collector trays with my concept on them. I liked the idea and agreed to do the painting. It was about that time that it was suggested that I should become a licensee myself and produce fine-art prints to sell to the Coca-Cola system.

As if struck by lightning, I suddenly realized I needed to join forces with Coca-Cola. I reacted to the opportunity immediately. An attorney at Coca-Cola took me under his wing and guided me through the licensee application process. We became good friends and remain so today. Becoming a Coca-Cola licensee in 1995 was a major positive step in my art career. It opened doors otherwise not available to me and has extended by many years my long connection to the company trademark.

The legal and licensing staff immediately seemed pleased to have me producing fine-art prints under a formal agreement, and ours began to sell well in the expanded market that we now reached. I started to envision other products that I would like approved. Notecards were a natural and easy to add. The idea of a gift calendar was an awesome undertaking. I would have to paint twelve images a year, and I would need to be able to distribute fairly large numbers to make it financially feasible.

The cost of producing the calendar was to be a substantial financial risk. I felt I could do it, and I was determined. It required additional guarantees to Coca-Cola and a commitment to print 20,000 calendars the first year. I did it and also produced a successful Christmas card at the same time.

Jim Harrison Coca-Cola art was well received, and I became well known within the Coca-Cola system and the Collector Club. I spoke at numerous club meetings and produced commemorative prints for special occasions. There were other companies approved to distribute licensed products to the system, and I aligned myself with them. As I became known to other licensees, many of them began using our images on their various products. Sunbelt Marketing, the Tin Box Company, Bertels, Conimar, Scene Weavers, Manual Weavers, Gloria and Pat, Keller Charles, Springbrook Puzzles, Cornell Steins, Evergreen Enterprises, and Giftco produced a variety of items, and I enjoyed a very nice income from the hundreds of pieces being sold all over the country.

I was also looking for opportunities for broad distribution for the products I was producing. Cracker Barrel was a good fit for us, and I had a nice relationship with them for years. They sold thousands of our calendars while they were in a licensee relationship with Coca-Cola. QVC was also a huge opportunity for me, and I loaded two of their big trucks with inventory headed to their warehouse. I was enjoying the benefits of our relationship with Coca-Cola, and I had to increase our staff to include a sales representative for wholesale and the Coca-Cola system.

Our activity in the Atlanta Mart was increasing, and for several years I had rep groups in the major markets in the United States. I was working quite hard, and business was growing, but I could begin to feel that we were overextending ourselves in the various distribution efforts. So I made a decision to downsize our Coca-Cola distribution efforts and a conscious effort to focus more on our Denmark Gallery retail possibilities. Coca-Cola has continued to give me national exposure, and we receive orders from all over the country and world. Jim Harrison Gallery frequently gets visitors who are aware of our work because of the Coca-Cola licensed products. Our relationship with Coca-Cola continues to be very good for me.

I once had a goal of surpassing the number of originals that Haddon Sundblom had painted for the Coca-Cola Company. He had created more than 150 images between 1931 and 1965. I now am reconciled that I will not reach that number, but I am comfortable knowing that I will probably hold the second-place spot with around 100 Coca-Cola paintings completed and approved during my career. I am making no record claims here other than having enjoyed a wonderful bunch of years associated with the most recognized icon in the world, perhaps longer than anyone else. Over 60 years have passed, and I am still eagerly pressing myself to get the next Coca-Cola Calendar cover finished in time for production to start. I always look forward to the next one and then the next one.

### Looking Backward and Forward

I have seen many changes in my sixty-five year relationship with the Coca-Cola trademark, and yet the red and white Spenserian logo has never changed. The icon of my youth, the same icon we see today, still sends out the same message all over the world to the millions of people who instantly recognize it. It suggests to everyone that they should pause from the day's efforts and be refreshed with the ice-cold drink. The message is simple, and it is spread in many different languages around the globe. From my youthful days in the 1950s, when I was watching the bottling process through the Denmark Coca-Cola plant window, to visits to the World of Coke or the Coca-Cola Corporate headquarters in Atlanta, I have a very broad overview of the past and glimpses into the future. I like to keep one foot in the door behind me and yet the other foot ready to step forward through the door to the future.

Writing this text has been most enjoyable. I have gone over the past half century, reminiscing and remembering those days of youthful anticipation and youthful energy. The slow days were filled with wishful dreams and lofty goals that seemed so far away. Yet, as the calendar pages slowly turned, the accomplishments began to fall into place although sometimes tinged with the disappointments that come with progress. I can recall the details from decades ago and even the emotions and senses that characterized those moments. There were the frustrating moments of failure and the confident ones of success.

In challenging and discouraging times, I well remember Mr. Cornforth pounding into me that it would get better and that things would change. Additionally I heard the same advice from others, and now in hindsight I can verify the truth in it. Of the many changes none is more drastic than those that have taken place in the art of making signs. Hand lettering is now replaced by a computer driven vinyl cutter. Software allows the sign designer simply to stretch the height or width of letters to fit the spaces. The art and the skill are in the manipulation of the computer programs and not the handling of a lettering quill brush. Spacing is automatically taken care of as the letters are typed. We did all of that in the old days by eyeing it in.

Coca-Cola collectibles are a story within themselves. Common sense pushed me in the direction of accumulating things from the past. I have a passion for keeping everything, and my several warehouses full of things attest to that smartness or sickness depending on whose interpretation you choose to listen to. My judgment has been reinforced by an overview of many years and a degree of scientific reasoning. Some time ago I needed an older version of the Coca-Cola can as a model for a painting. Not having one at hand, Margaret found and purchased the desired can, which was about 20 years old at the time. She had to pay 42 dollars for it. My collector's reasoning is that all well-kept Coca-Cola cans will appreciate in value over the years.

Thus I have hundreds of cans in many versions in large cardboard boxes in my warehouse. The passing of time and the vision of the owners in the future will answer the question of my wisdom in holding onto the cans and my many other items of the past.

So it has been my nature to look backward and to look forward at the same time. It is truly possible to experience melancholy and enjoy gleefulness simultaneously. Such is my bittersweet mood as I bring this writing to a pause, not a stop. Closing this chapter is only an opportunity to open the next. ●

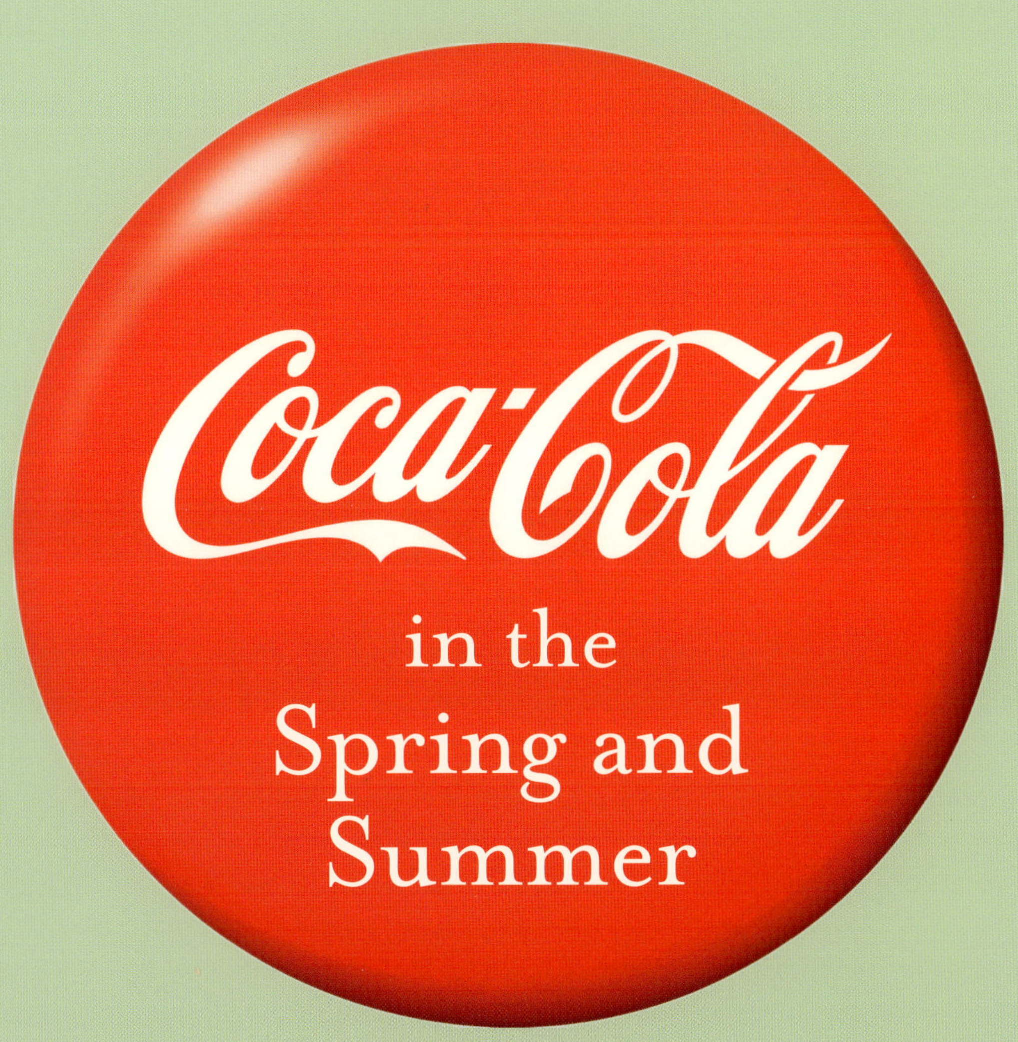
Coca-Cola
in the
Spring and
Summer

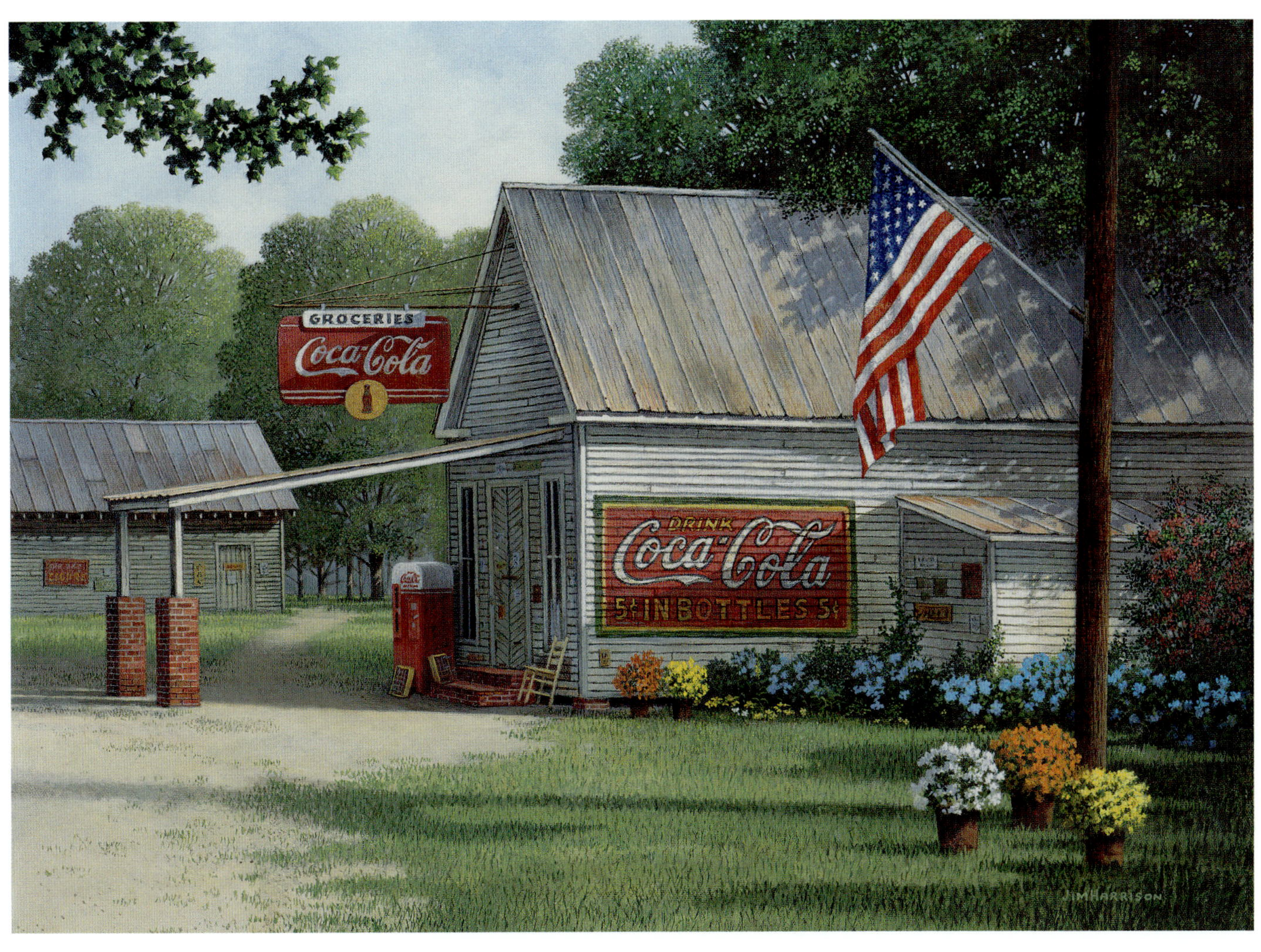


*The Flag and Coca-Cola*

ACRYLIC ON CANVAS, 18 × 24 INCHES, 2002

No discussion of American business history can overlook the success of the Coca-Cola Company, the ultimate example of the American dream. No other corporation or product can match it. For almost a century, ice-cold Coca-Cola has been the universal thirst quencher and one of the world's best-known American products. Coca-Cola's trademark has been a favorite subject of mine throughout my life. I jokingly have said that I have worked for Coca-Cola for more than sixty years, most likely longer than any other employee there.

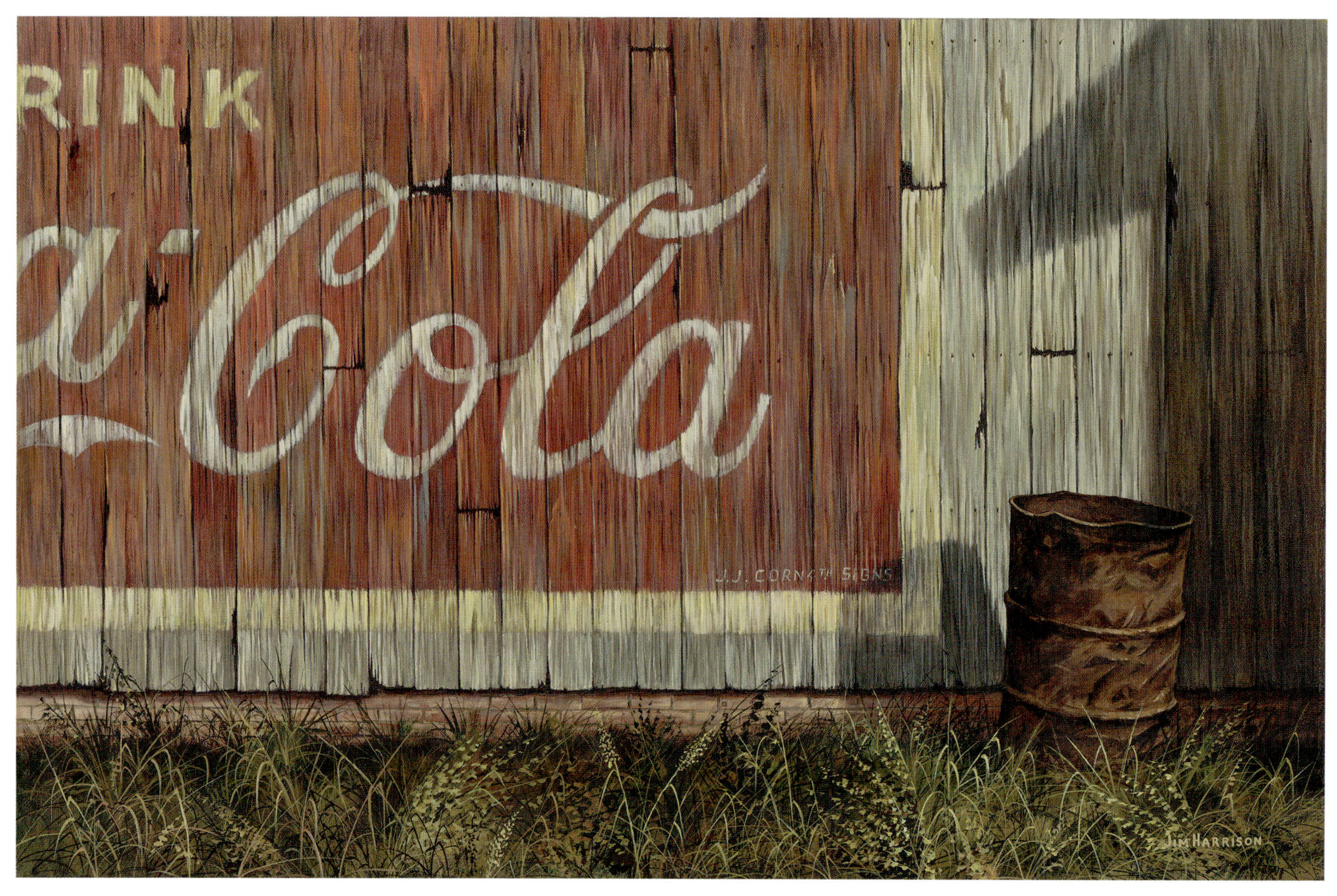


*J. J. Cornforth*

ACRYLIC ON CANVAS, 20 × 30 INCHES, 1975

Mr. Cornforth signed his signs J. J. Corn4th Signs.

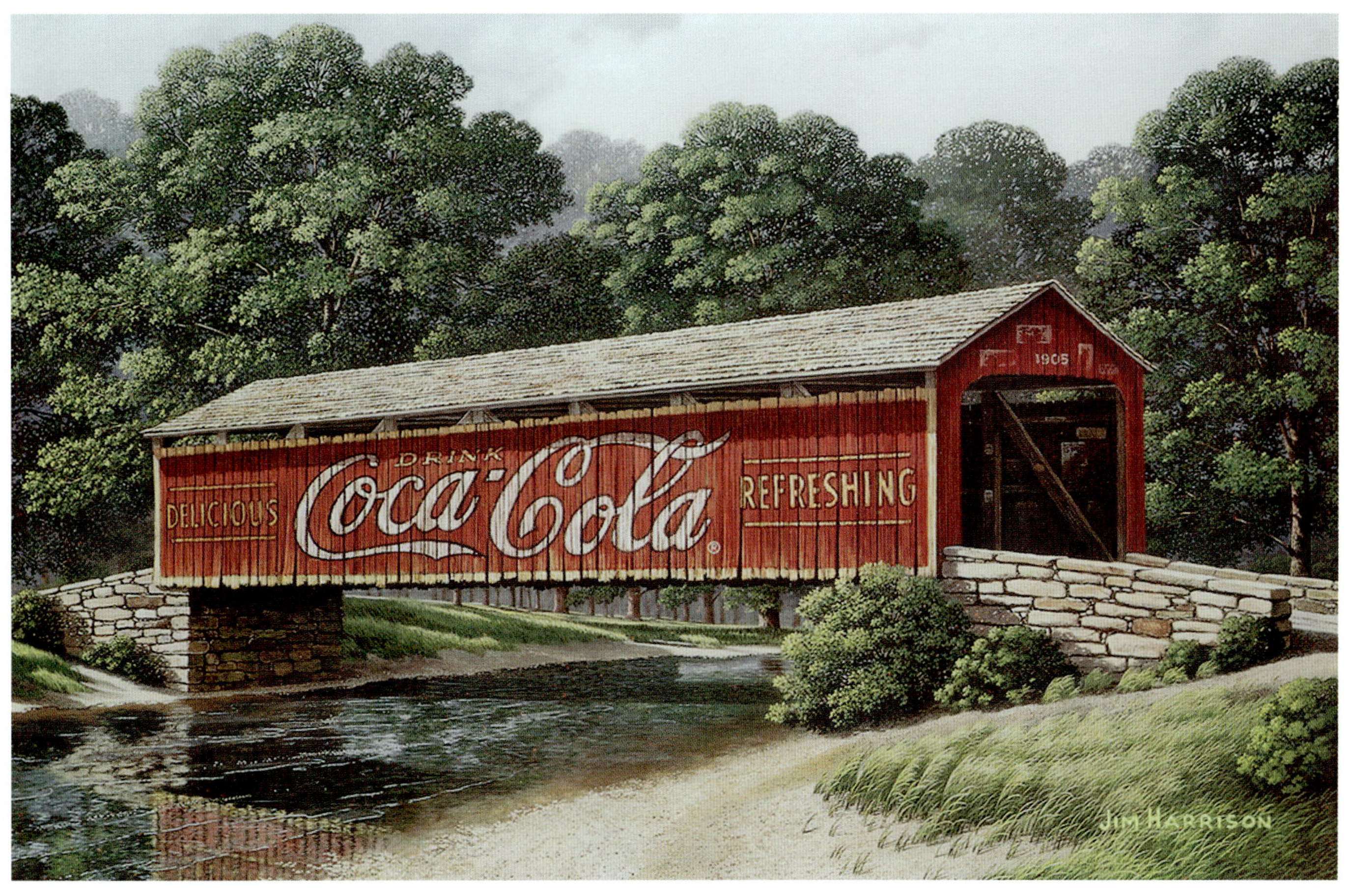


*Summer Coca-Cola Bridge*

ACRYLIC ON CANVAS, 24 × 36 INCHES, 1995

I love covered bridges and visit one every chance I get. It certainly is like stepping into the past. Mr. Cornforth and I never painted a sign on one. I am not sure just how they employ scaffolding to reach and work on the side, but it has always fascinated me.

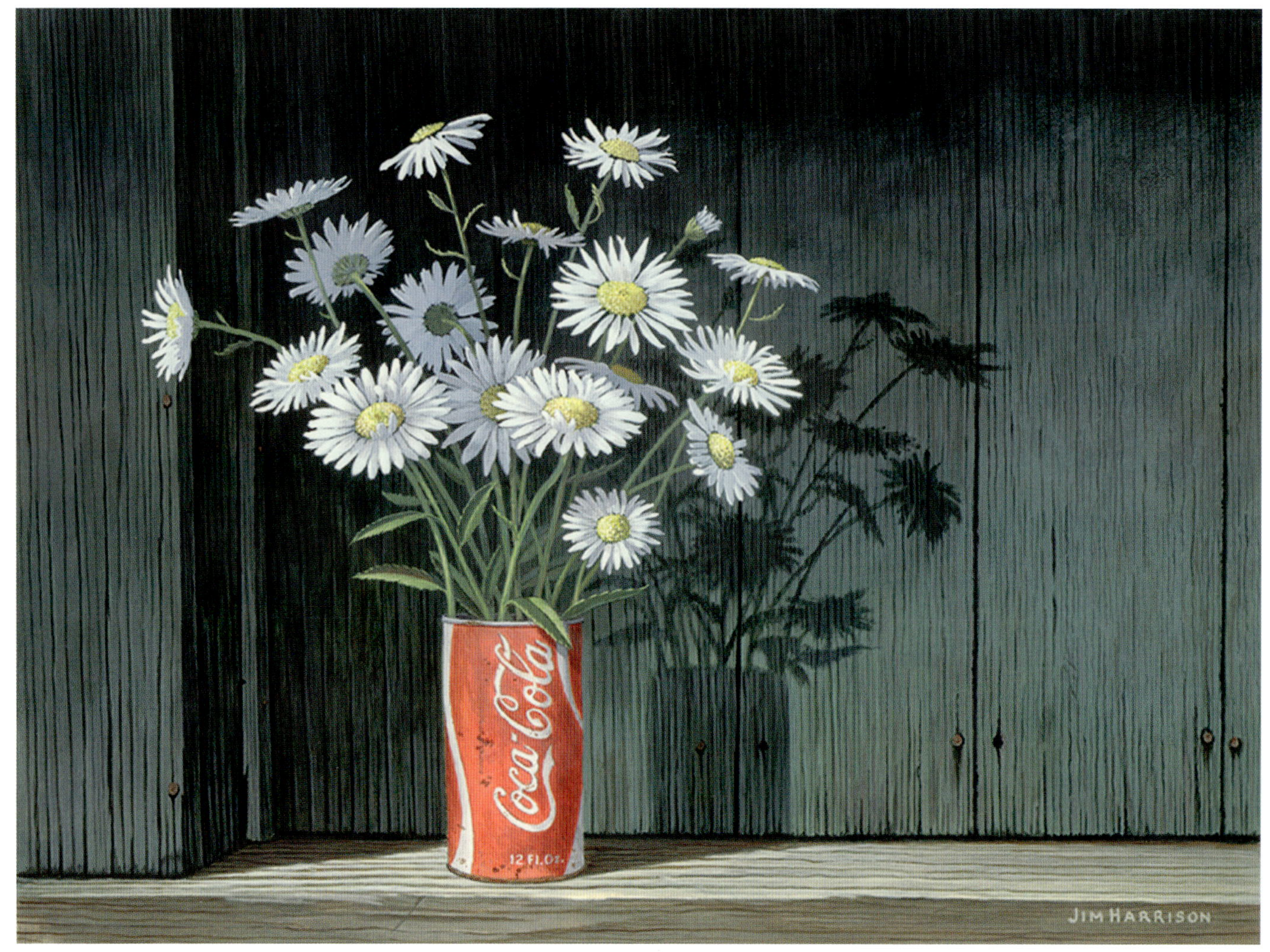


*Coca-Cola Can with Daisies*

ACRYLIC ON ILLUSTRATION BOARD, 12 × 16 INCHES, 1997

Even a rusted can becomes an object of beauty when struck by sunlight. The arrangement of light and shadow enhances the most insignificant of things.

FACING *Coca-Cola Calendar Cover 2015*

ACRYLIC ON CANVAS, 12 × 16 INCHES, 2015

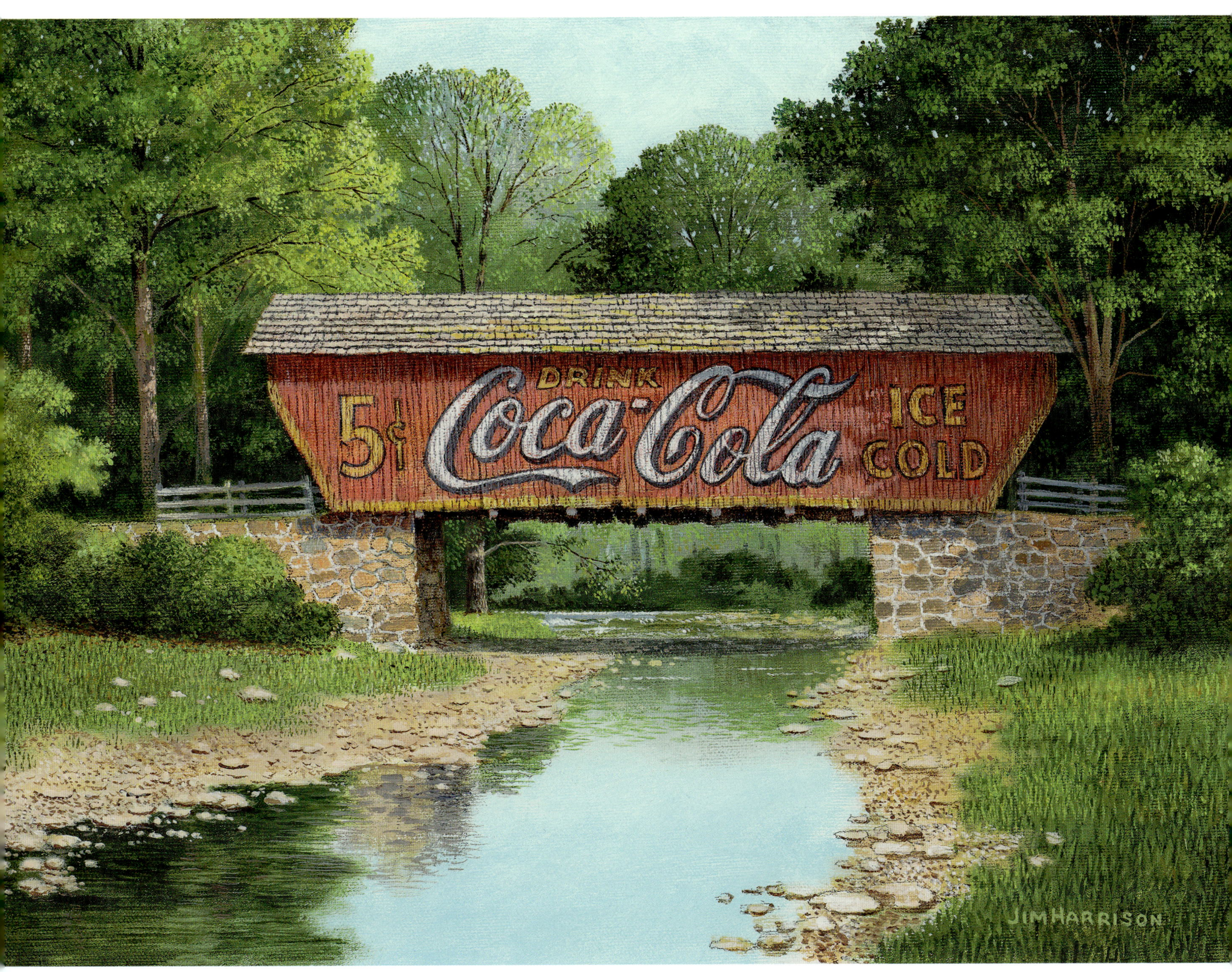
DRINK
Coca-Cola
5¢
ICE
COLD
JIM HARRISON

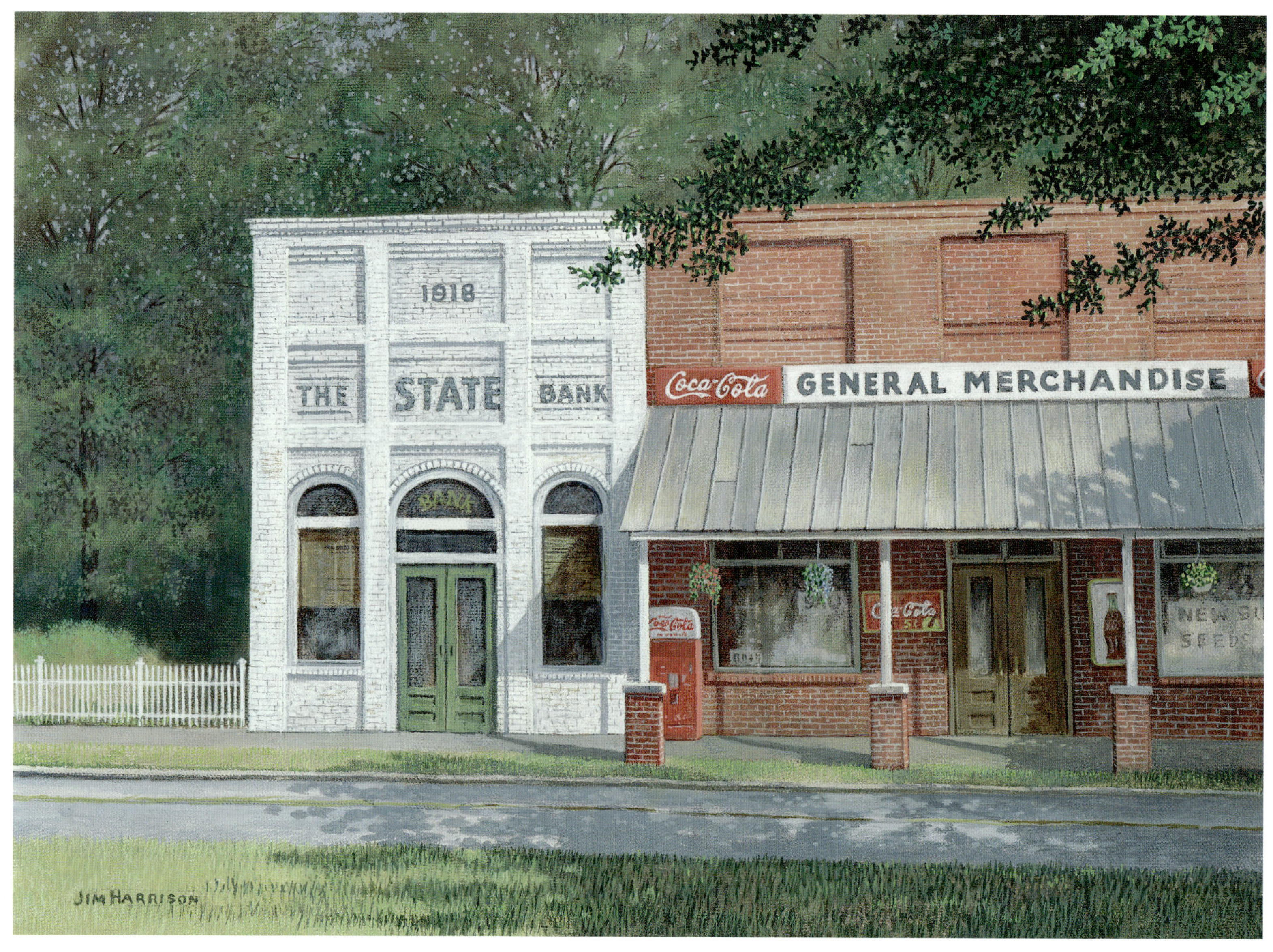


*August 2000*

ACRYLIC ON CANVAS, 12 × 16 INCHES, 1999

The Coca-Cola Company was a master at marketing. No small town was without the well-known symbol incorporated into the fabric of Main Street USA on its stores and businesses.

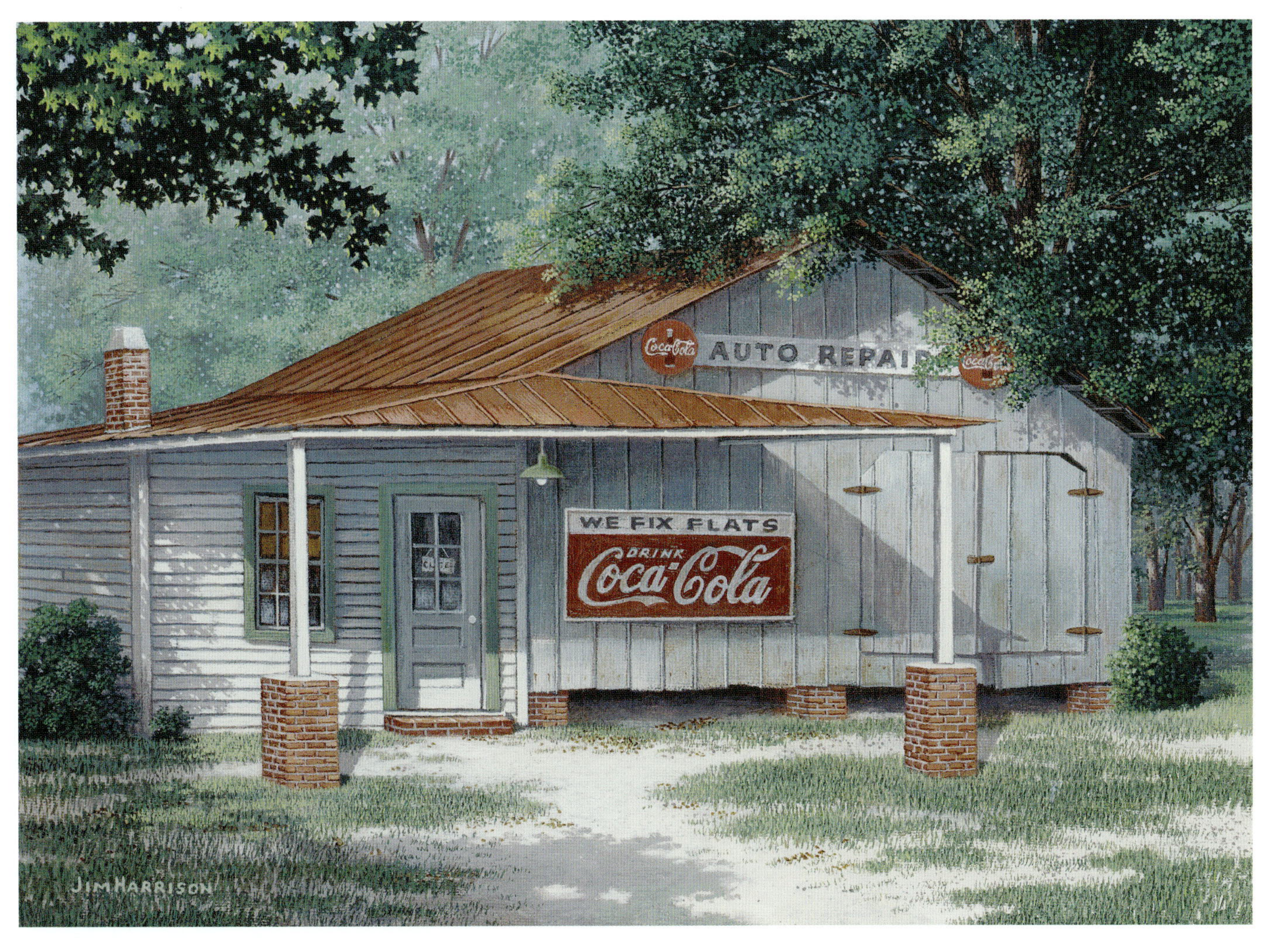


*August 2002*

ACRYLIC ON CANVAS, 12 × 16 INCHES, 1997

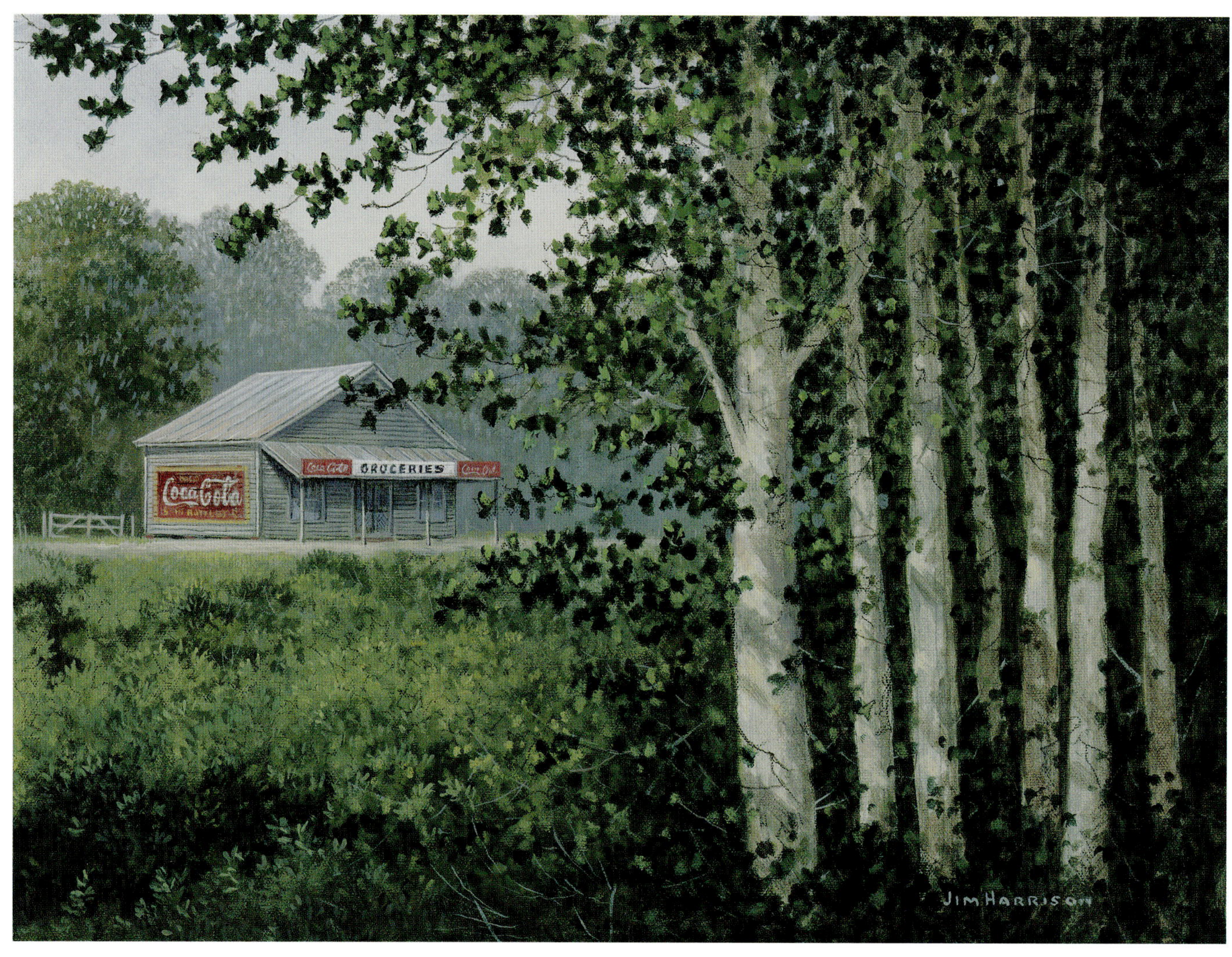


*August 2003*

ACRYLIC ON CANVAS, 14 × 18 INCHES, 2002

I love country stores. Not only are they rich with emotional associations. They are also an essential part of our past.

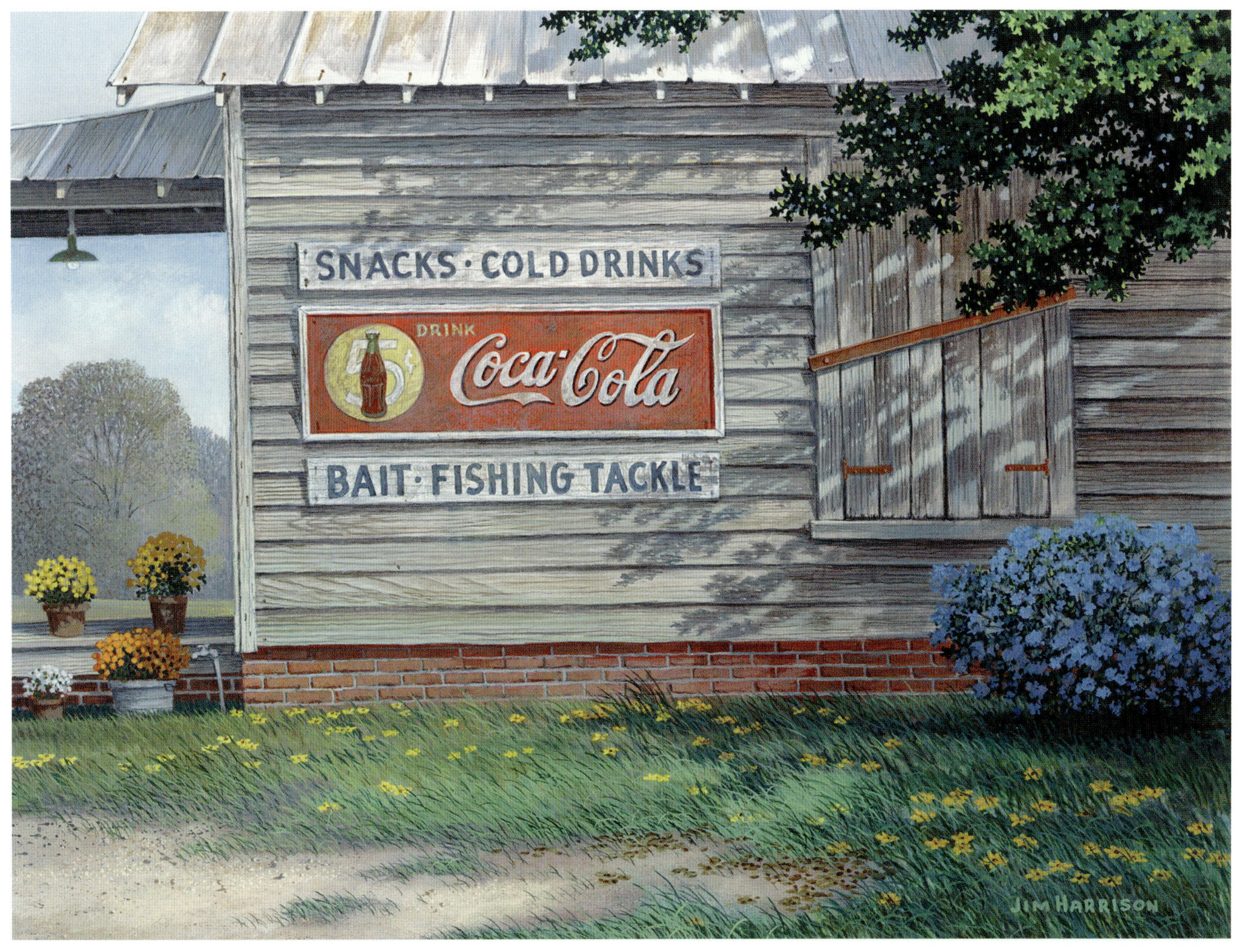


*Bait, Fishing, and Tackle*

ACRYLIC ON ILLUSTRATION BOARD, 11 × 14 INCHES, 1998

No fishing trip was complete without a Coca-Cola. Many a lazy afternoon could be spent stretched on the bank of a pond with your fishing pole in hand and an ice-cold Coke by your side.

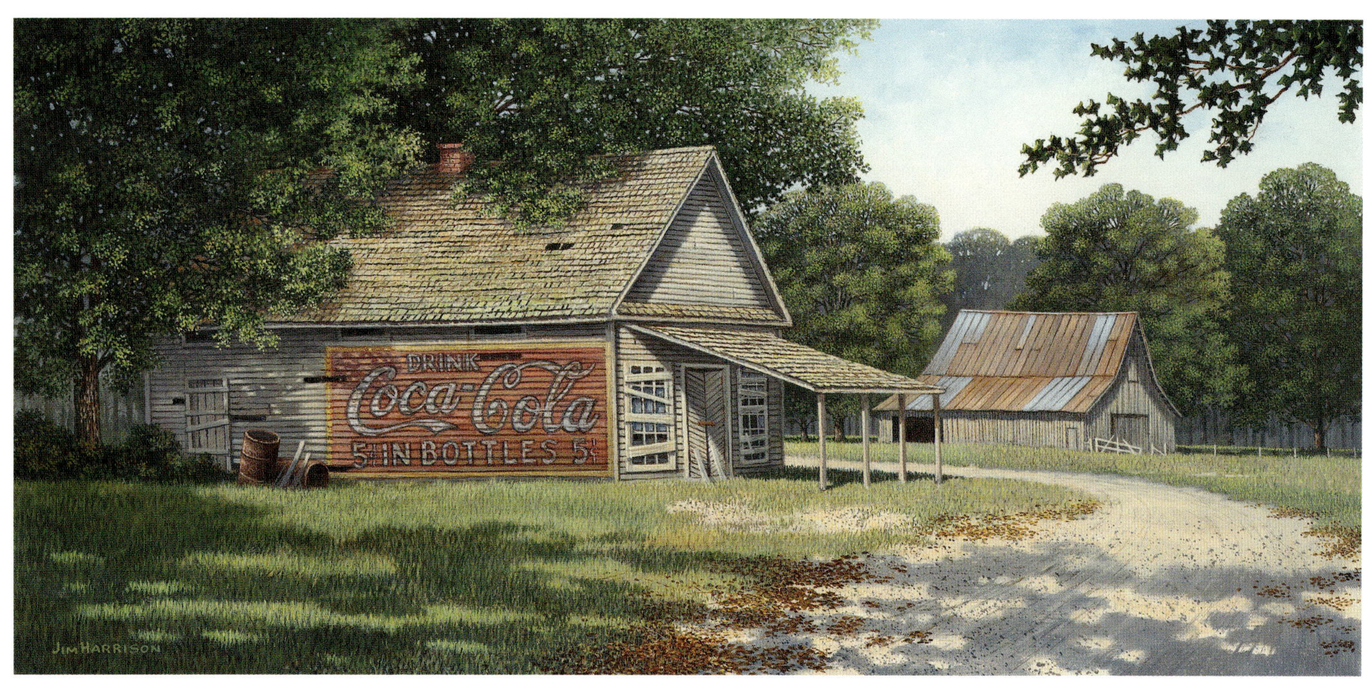


*Coca-Cola 5 Cent Bottles*

ACRYLIC ON ILLUSTRATION BOARD, 15 × 30 INCHES, 2006

I have visited this store many times. An elderly Mr. Luther owned the little grocery business, and I think he mainly kept it open just to have something to do. It is near the river and is a gathering place for the fishermen. I have painted a number of versions of the building in different seasons. When CNN did a documentary of my work, they filmed some footage inside of the store.

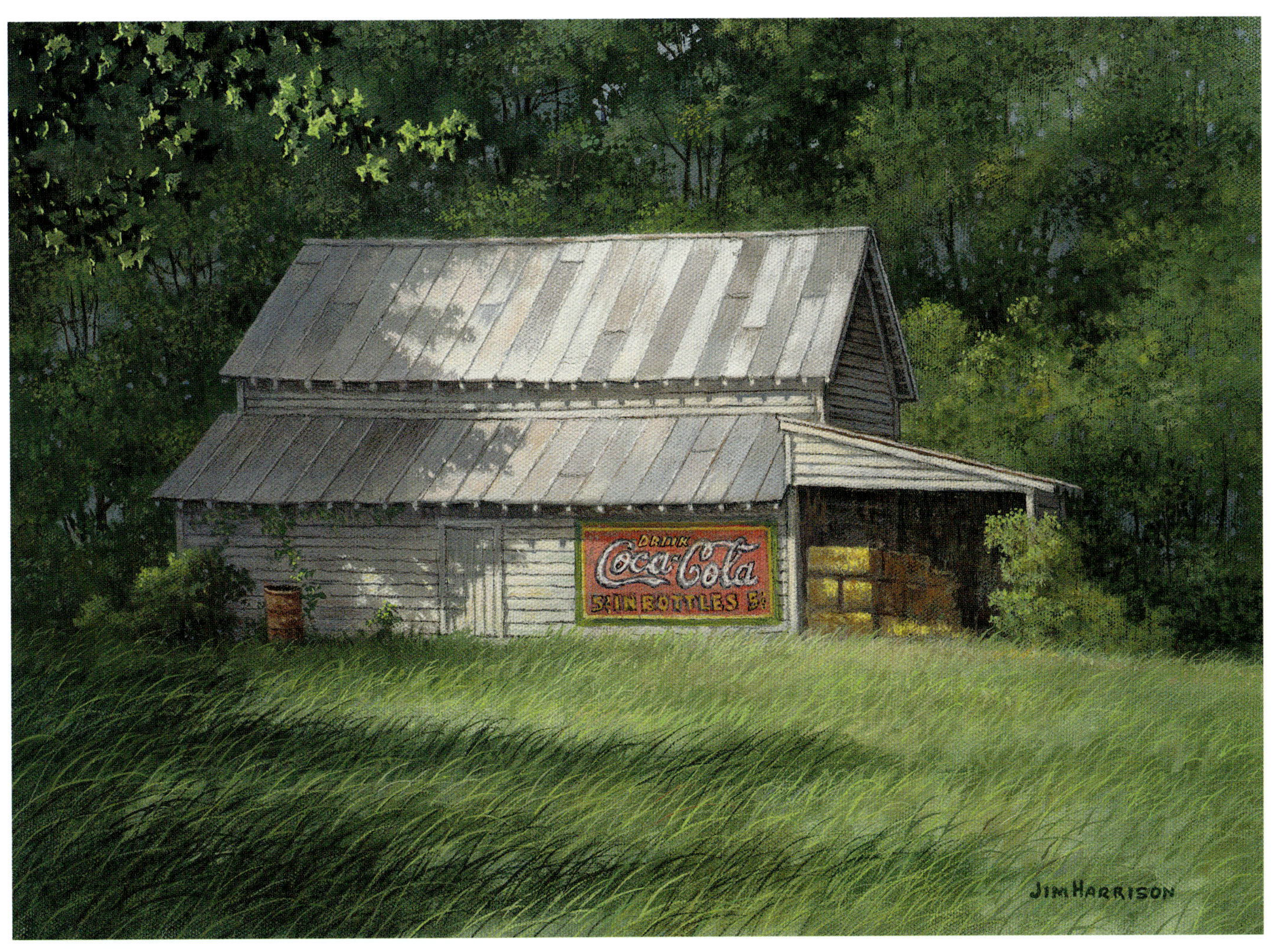


*Coca-Cola Barn 2008*

ACRYLIC ON CANVAS, 12 × 16 INCHES, 2007

Slowly the buildings are giving in to the thousands of summer suns and the freezing winter rains. Nestled in the grassless sand or propped upon hard, bare ground, long-abandoned country stores stand under huge old shade trees, their faded sides visually pealing out, "DRINK COCA-COLA." Appearing to have been part of the landscape forever, they have weathered and worn their way into a natural place in the surrounding environment. "It's been there just about as long as I can remember," an old-timer will say. "It goes a way back." The old edifices, well past their prime, are monuments to eras and temperaments long since gone from the commercial mainstream.

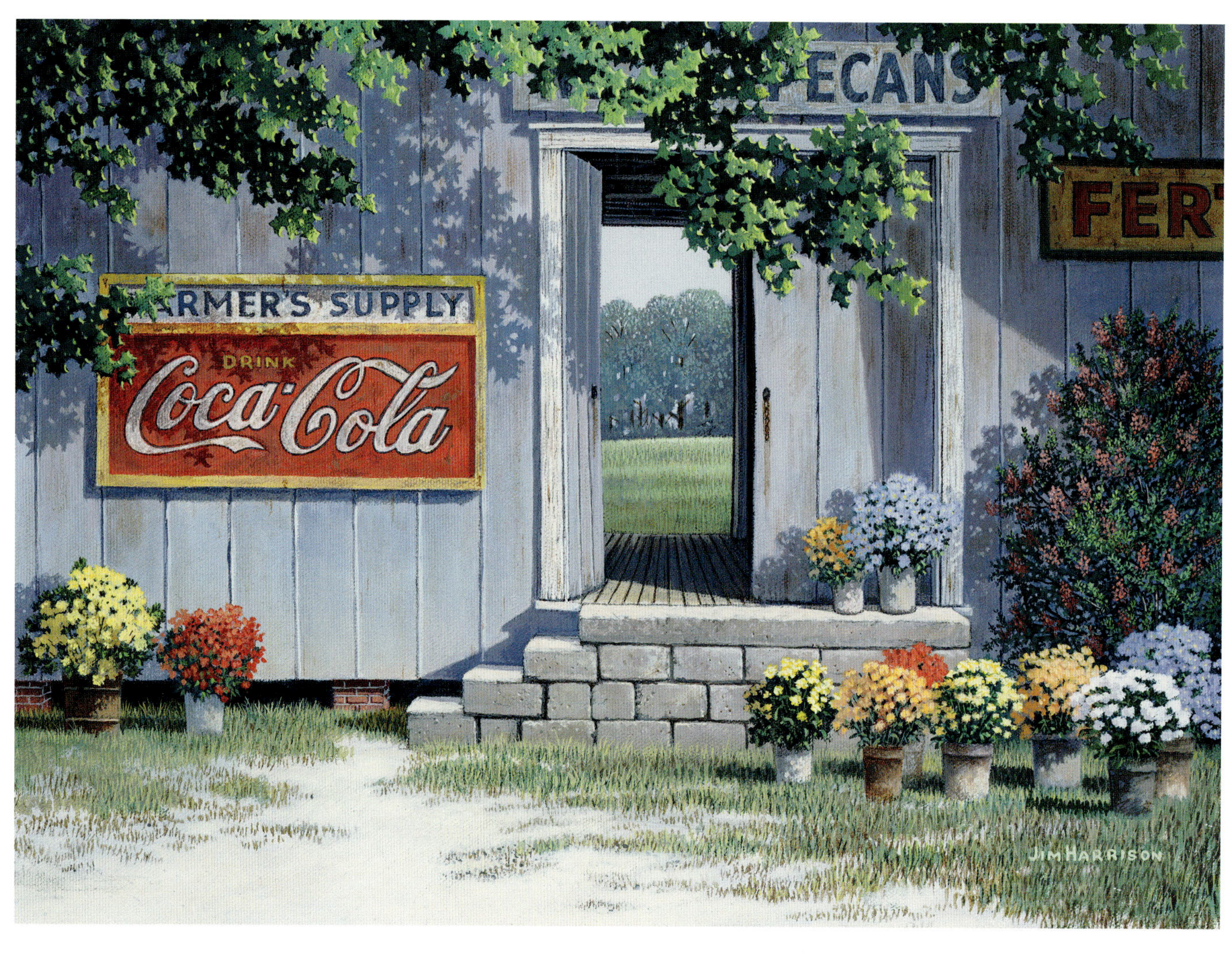


*Coca-Cola Farmers Supply*

ACRYLIC ON CANVAS, 12 × 16 INCHES, 1998

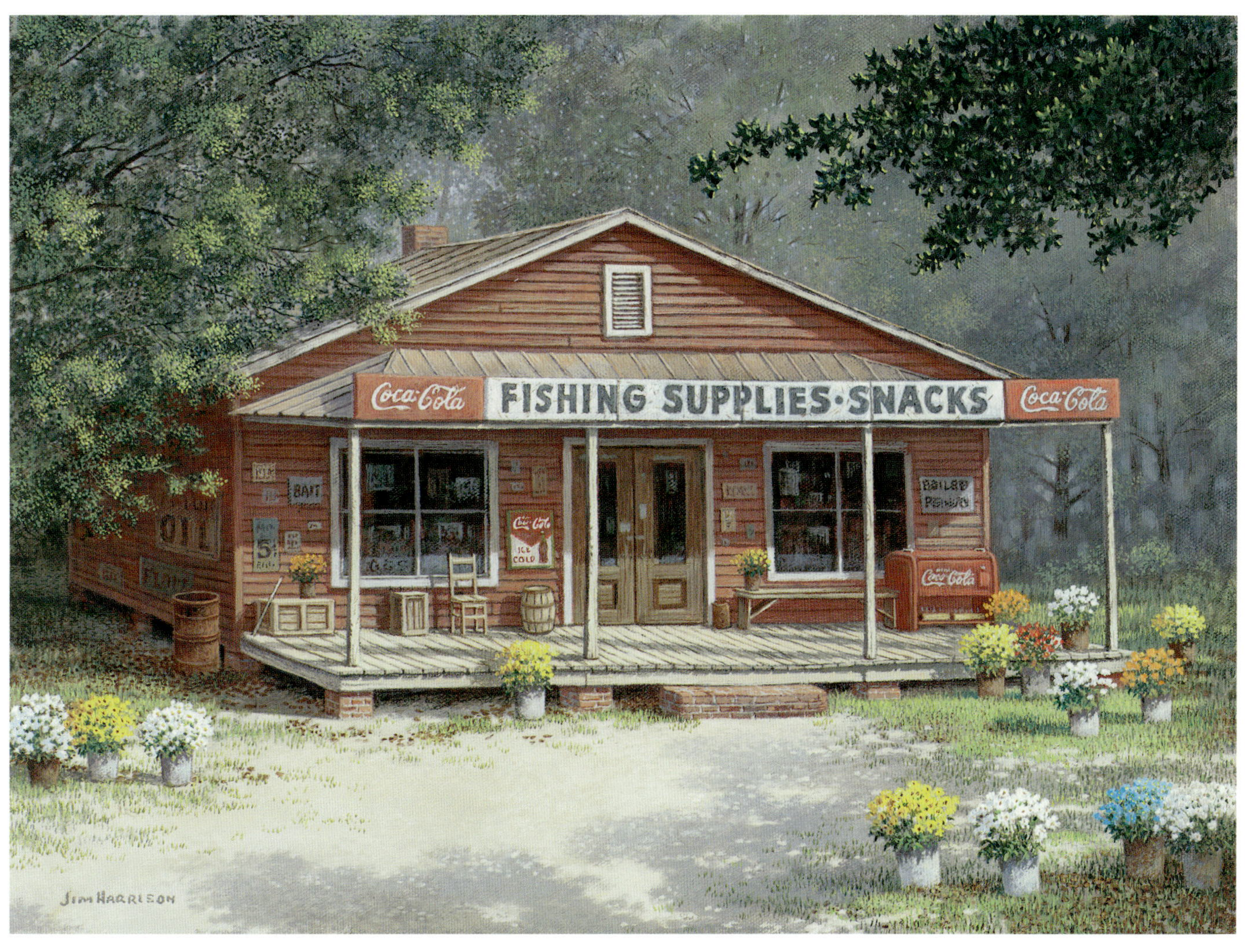


*Coca-Cola Fishing Supplies*

ACRYLIC ON CANVAS, 12 × 16 INCHES, 2001

A search for the real, American entrepreneurial spirit must not begin in the contemporary metropolitan offices of our giant corporations. No, not there. To learn of the development of the mercantile system in this country, once must pause, turn around, and take a backward look.

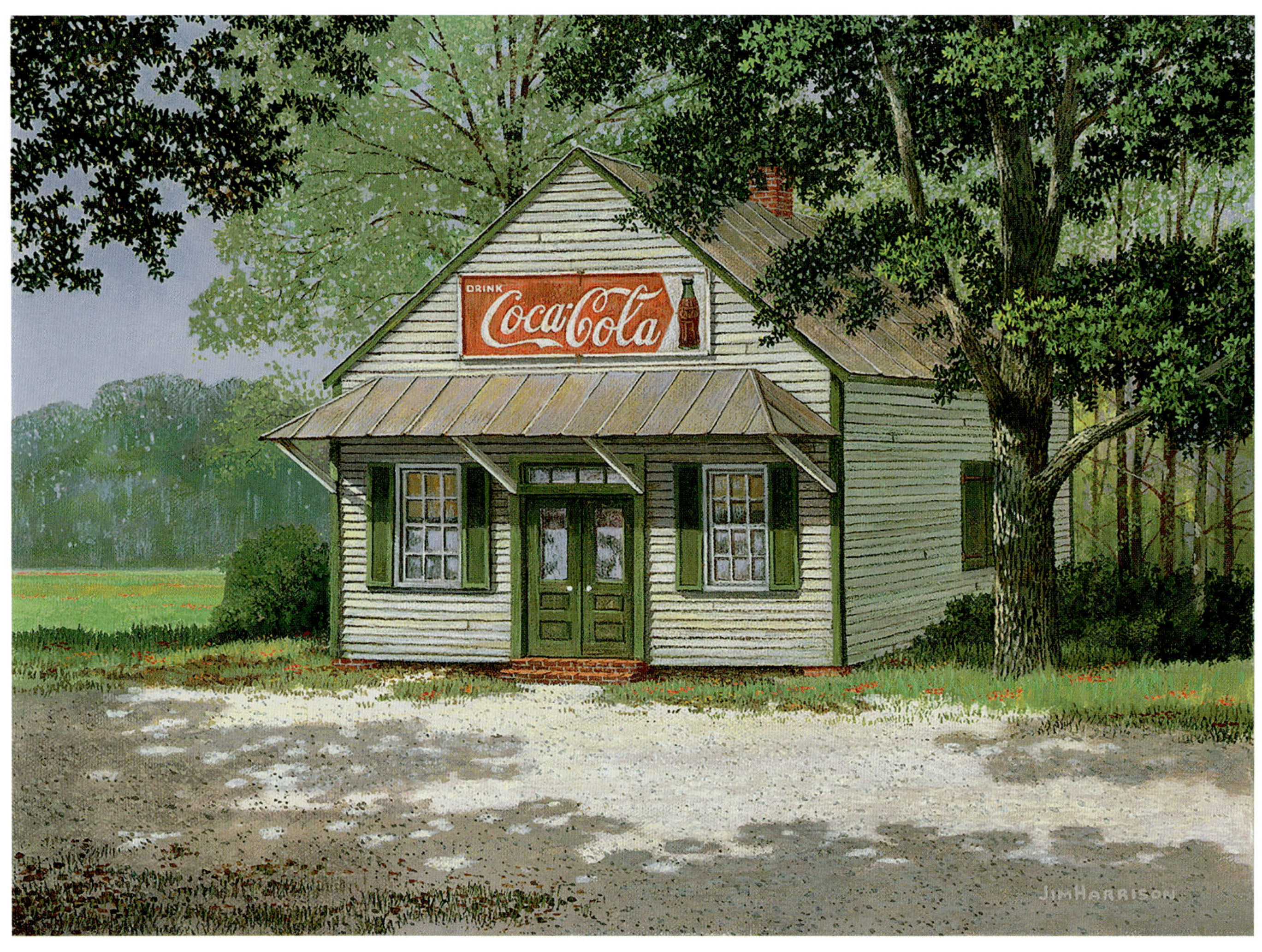


*Coca-Cola in May*

ACRYLIC ON CANVAS, 12 × 16 INCHES, 1996

Mr. Cornforth was very superstitious about the color green, and to my knowledge he never owned a can. He believed it was bad luck. When a sign job called for green, we always used yellow mixed with blue or black to make the color. I never knew why he felt that way, but to this day I mix all my greens from blues and yellows on my palette.

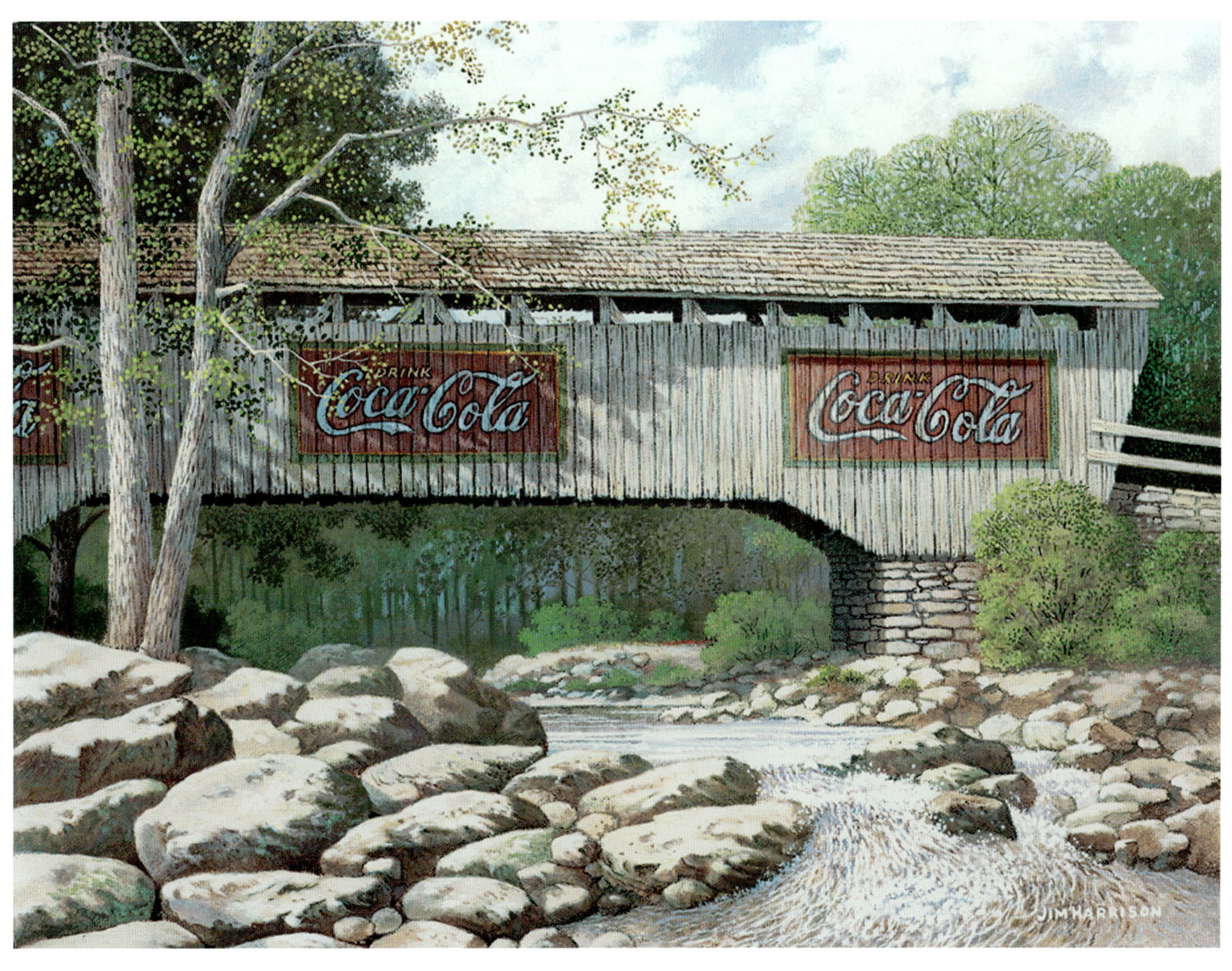


*Coca-Cola Bridge in May*

ACRYLIC ON CANVAS, 14 × 18 INCHES, 1988

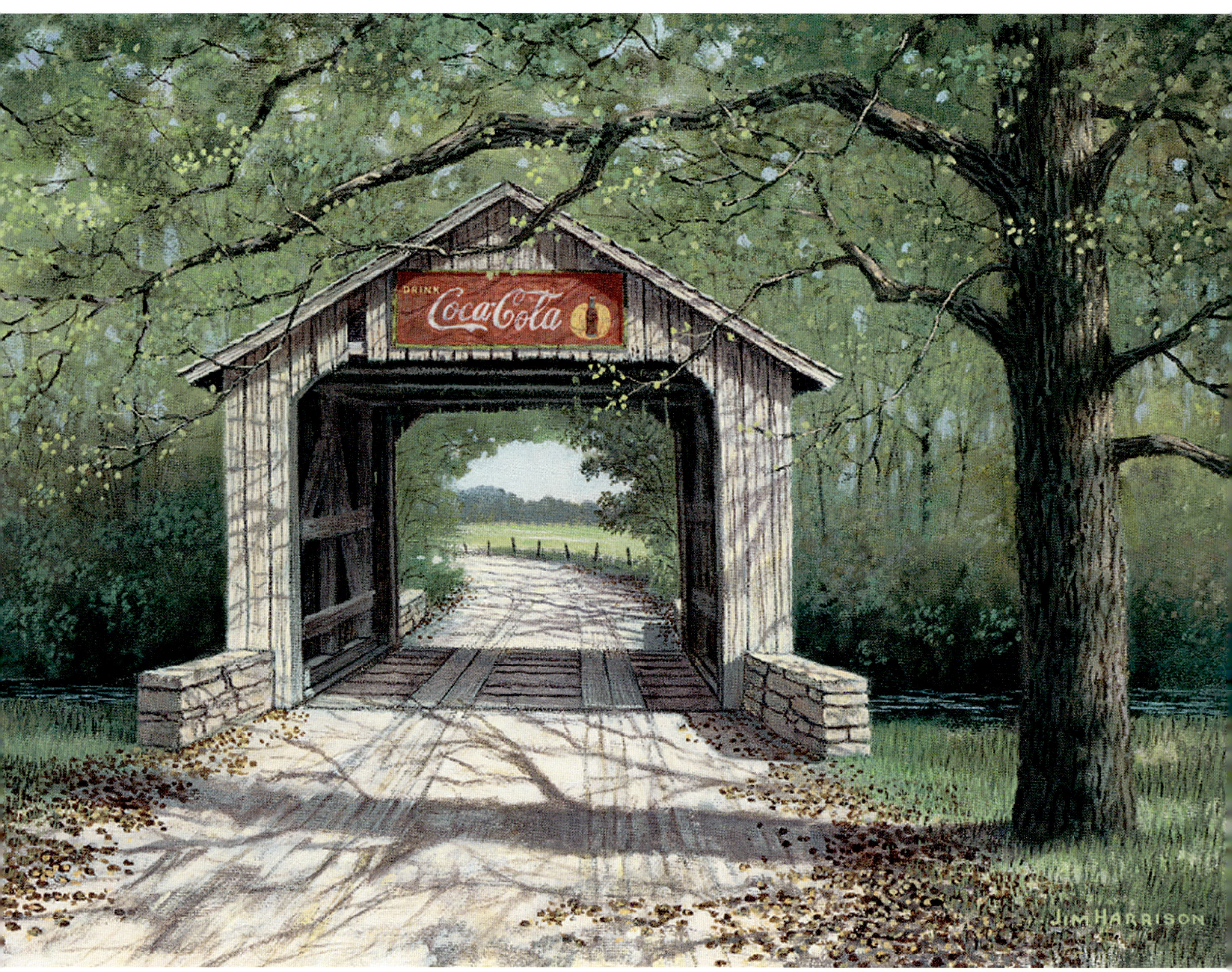
DRINK
Coca-Cola
JIM HARRISON

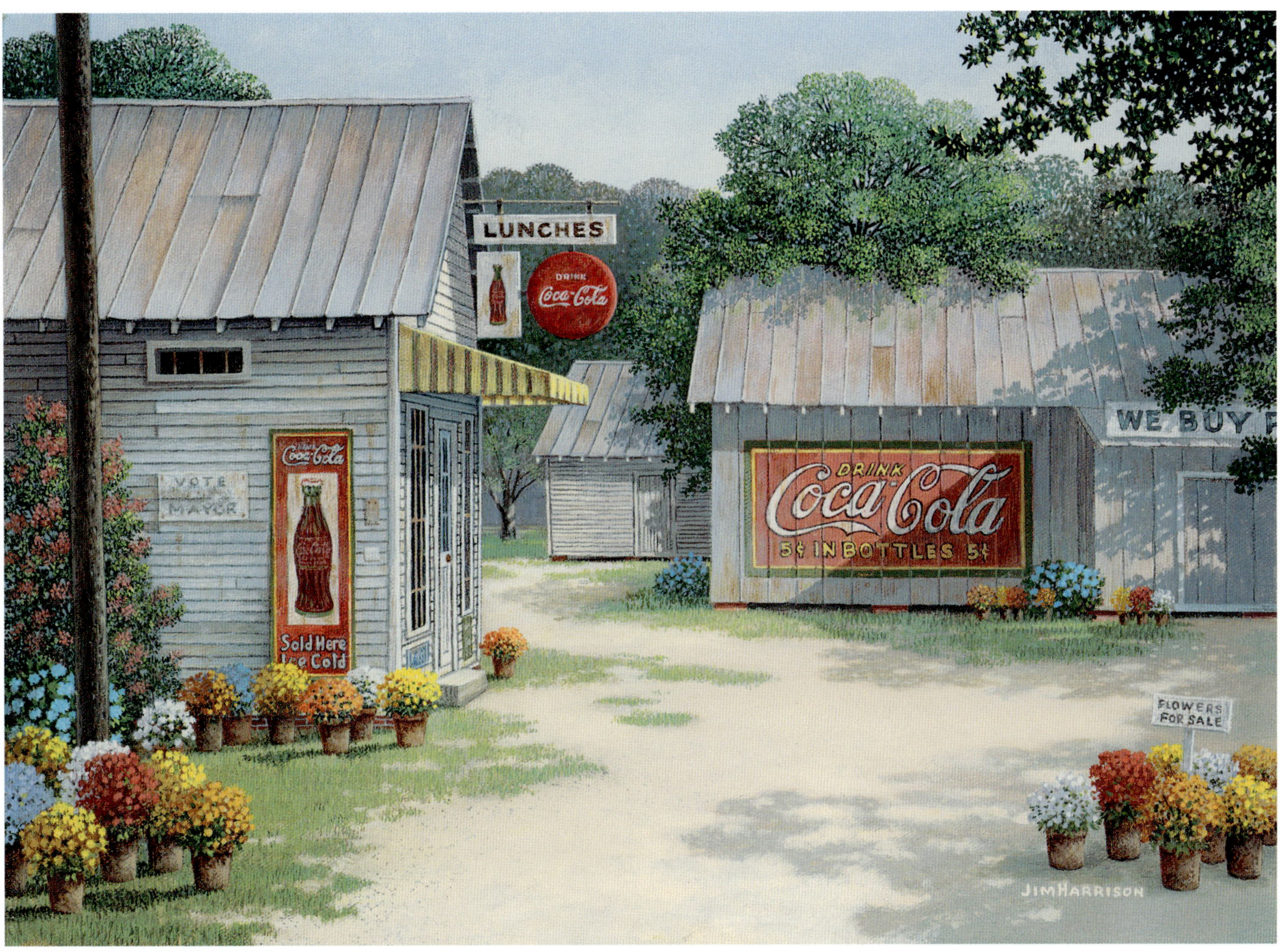


*Coca-Cola in Back Lot*

ACRYLIC ON CANVAS, 12 × 16 INCHES, 1998

One year the company included an 8-foot tin bottle in the wall-bulletin design. We did install those on the wall after we painted the rest of the sign background. Those old signs are sought after collectibles today. I know we must have thrown away several dozen of them.

FACING *Coca-Cola Bridge Over Creek*

ACRYLIC ON CANVAS, 12 × 16 INCHES, 1998

It's good for the soul to travel the unpaved roads of our rural countryside.

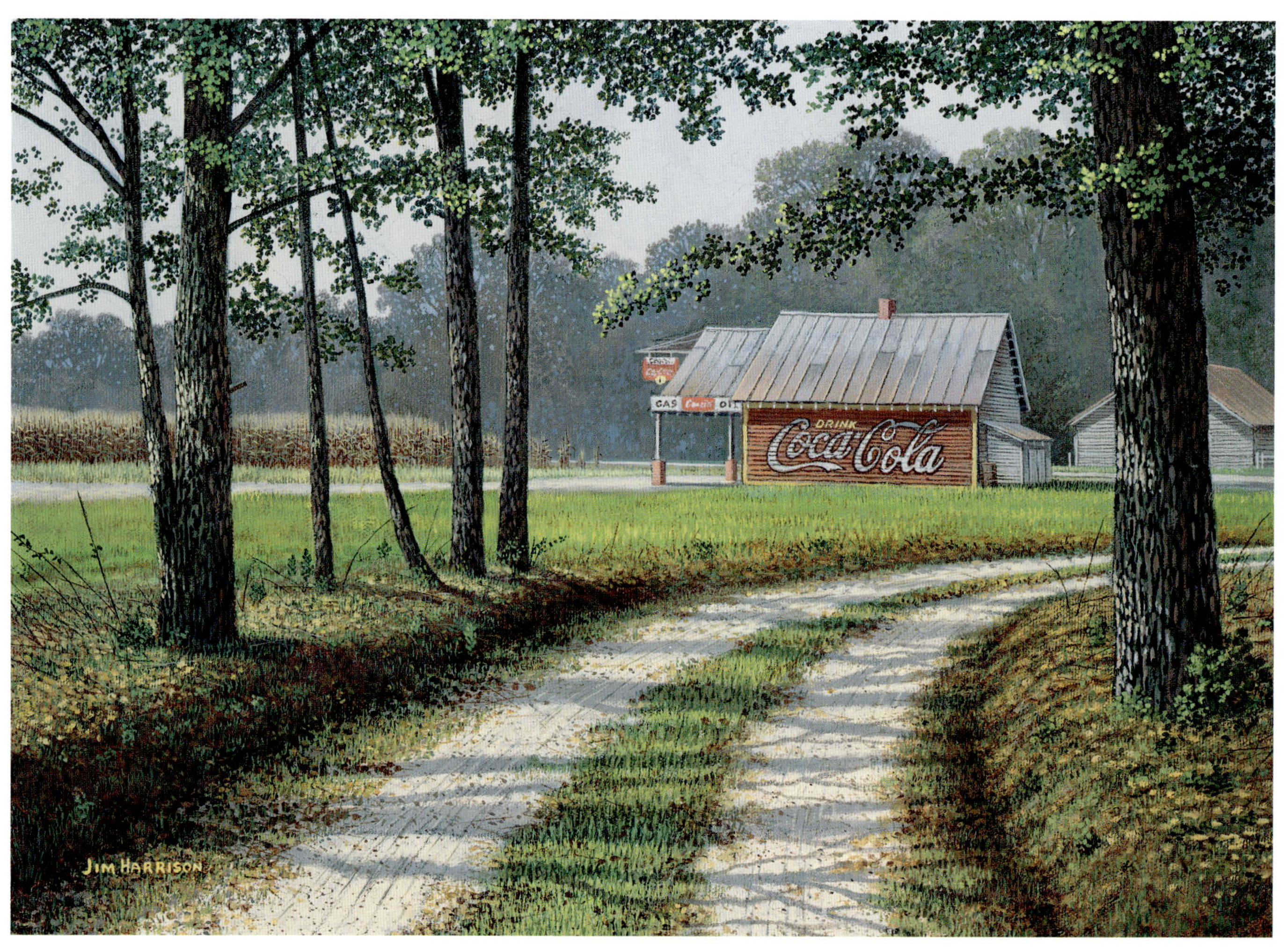


*Coca-Cola in the Country*

ACRYLIC ON CANVAS, 12 × 16 INCHES, 1998

In the early fifties, when I was fourteen years old and working as a sign-painting apprentice to J. J. Cornforth., we painted Coca-Cola signs on the outside walls of various country stores in and around my hometown of Denmark, South Carolina. I dreamed of doing two things: putting my name by Mr. Cornforth's on a Coca-Cola sign and painting the WELCOME TO DENMARK signs for the city. I never got a chance to do either.

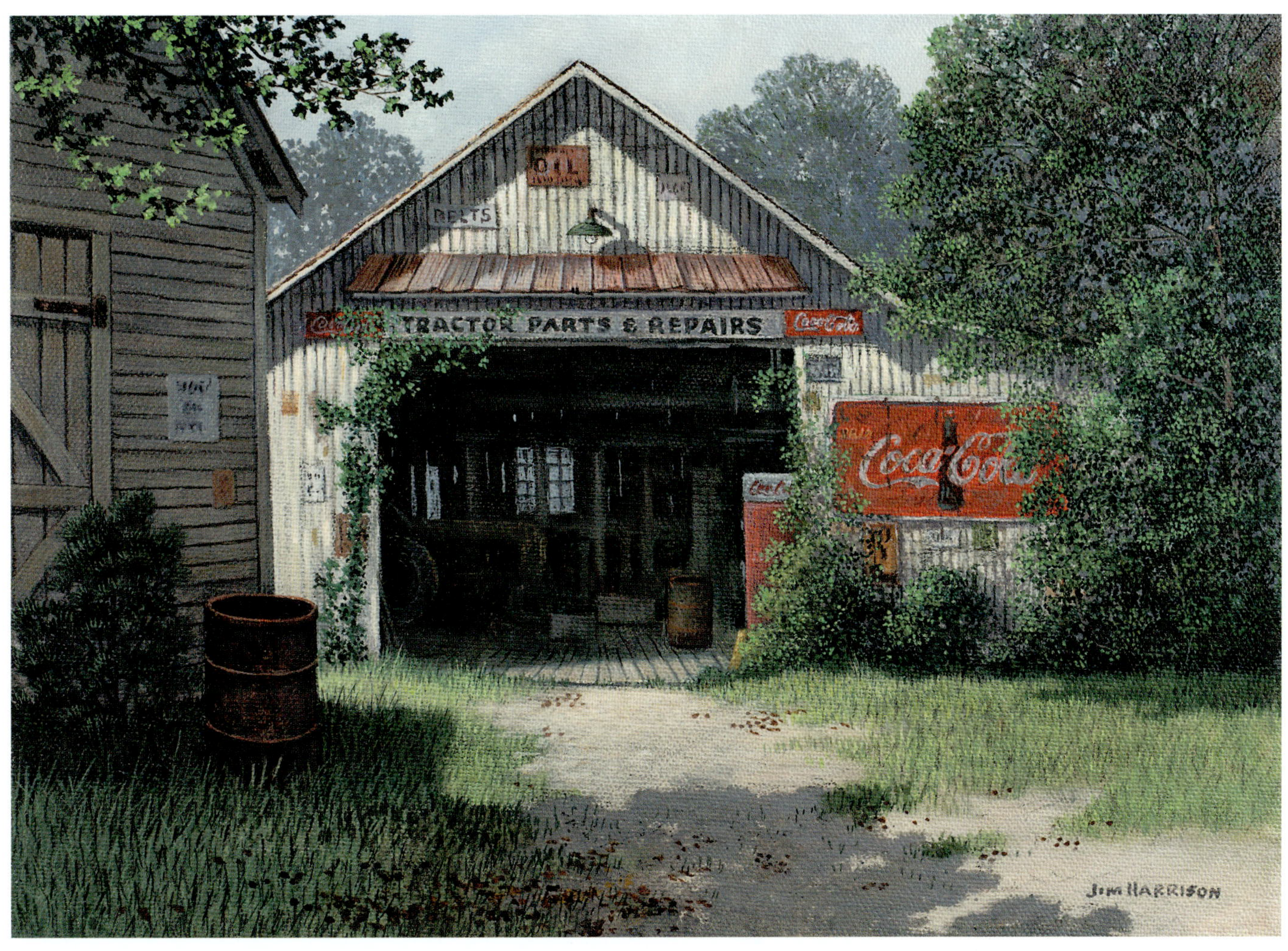


*Coca-Cola Tractor Parts*

ACRYLIC ON CANVAS, 9 × 12 INCHES, 2000

I'm an incurable collector of old signs. I have hundreds of them temporarily stored and displayed in the building next to my gallery. Almost daily someone wants to buy one, but they are not for sale. Collecting, like painting and writing, cannot be approached as a business. When I'm told of any old sign in this area, there is a consuming desire to get it. I must try to, and usually do, make it mine. A person who collects with profit in mind will never experience that kind of excitement and joy.

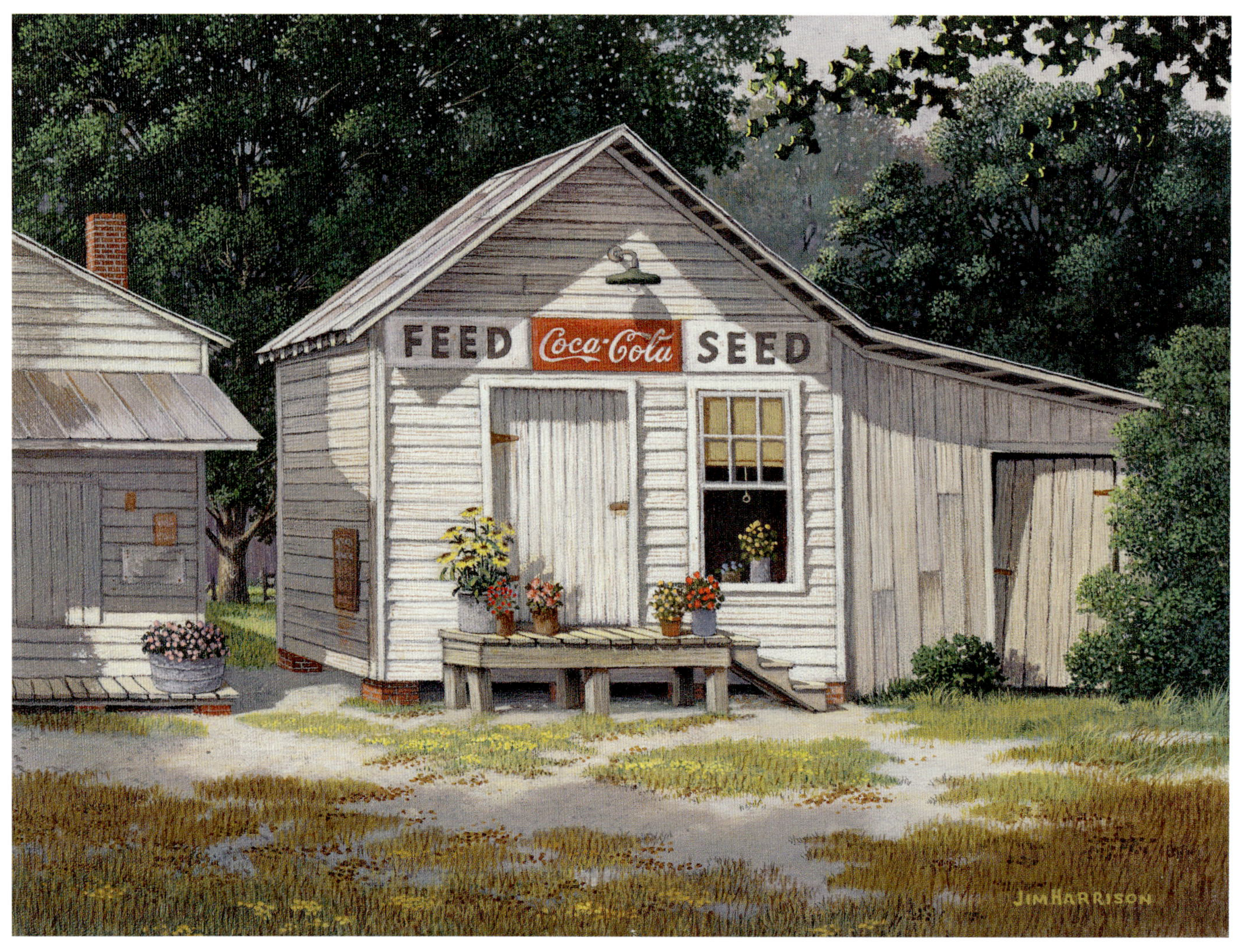


*Feed, Seed, and Coca-Cola*

ACRYLIC ON CANVAS, 14 × 18 INCHES, 1996

For more than half a century, I have had a love affair with old buildings, old things, and old ways.

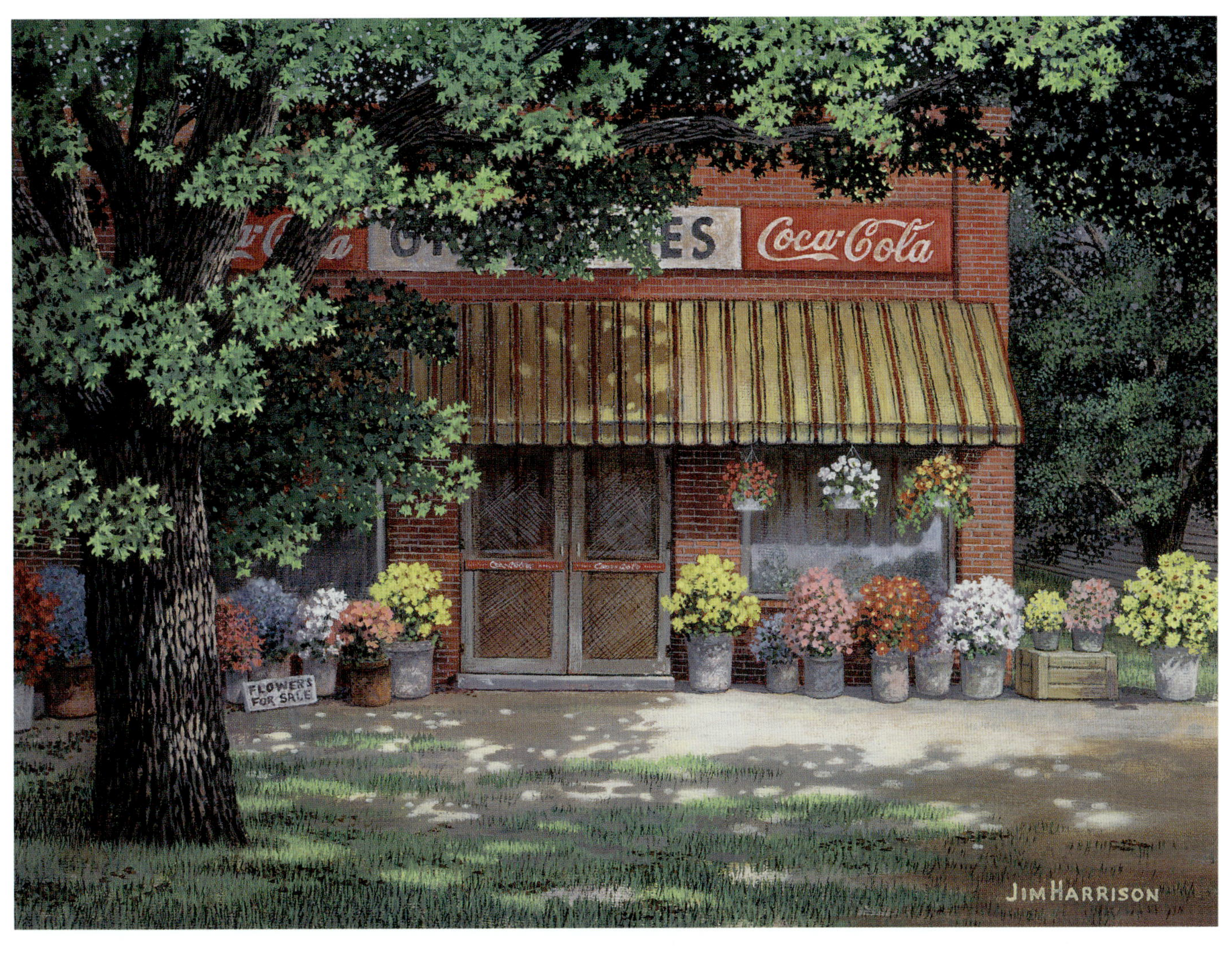


*April 2001*

ACRYLIC ON CANVAS, 12 × 16 INCHES, 1997

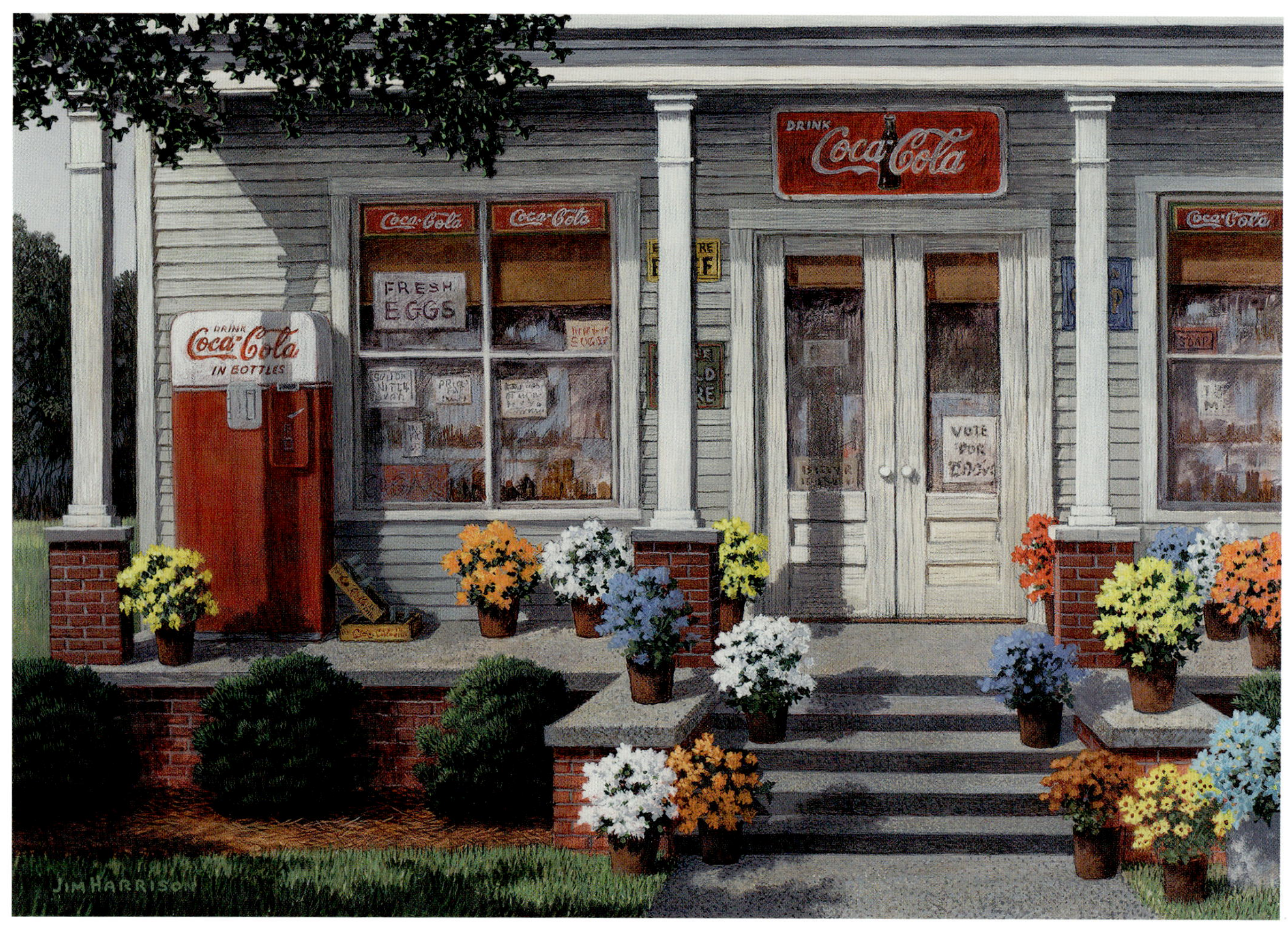


*July 2001*

ACRYLIC ON ILLUSTRATION BOARD, 10.5 × 15 INCHES, 2000

FACING *July 2002*

ACRYLIC ON CANVAS, 12 × 16 INCHES, 1996

Traveling through the countryside, one dirt road will eventually cross another. Though not easily recognized, at the crossing of the roads there may well be the remnants of a once-thriving country store. There within unpainted pine walls can be found the beginning of modern, enterprising America.

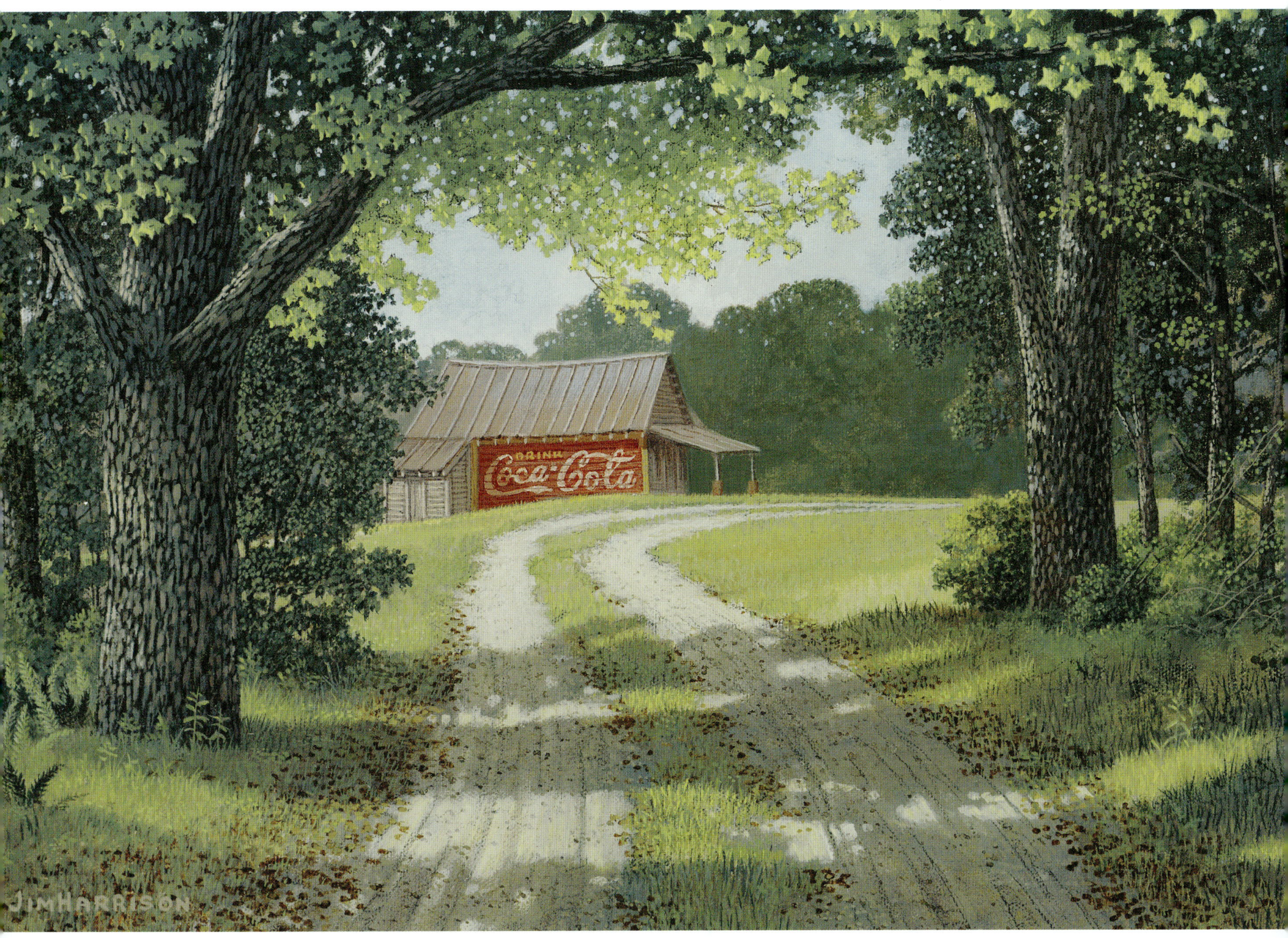
DRINK
Coca-Cola
JIM HARRISON

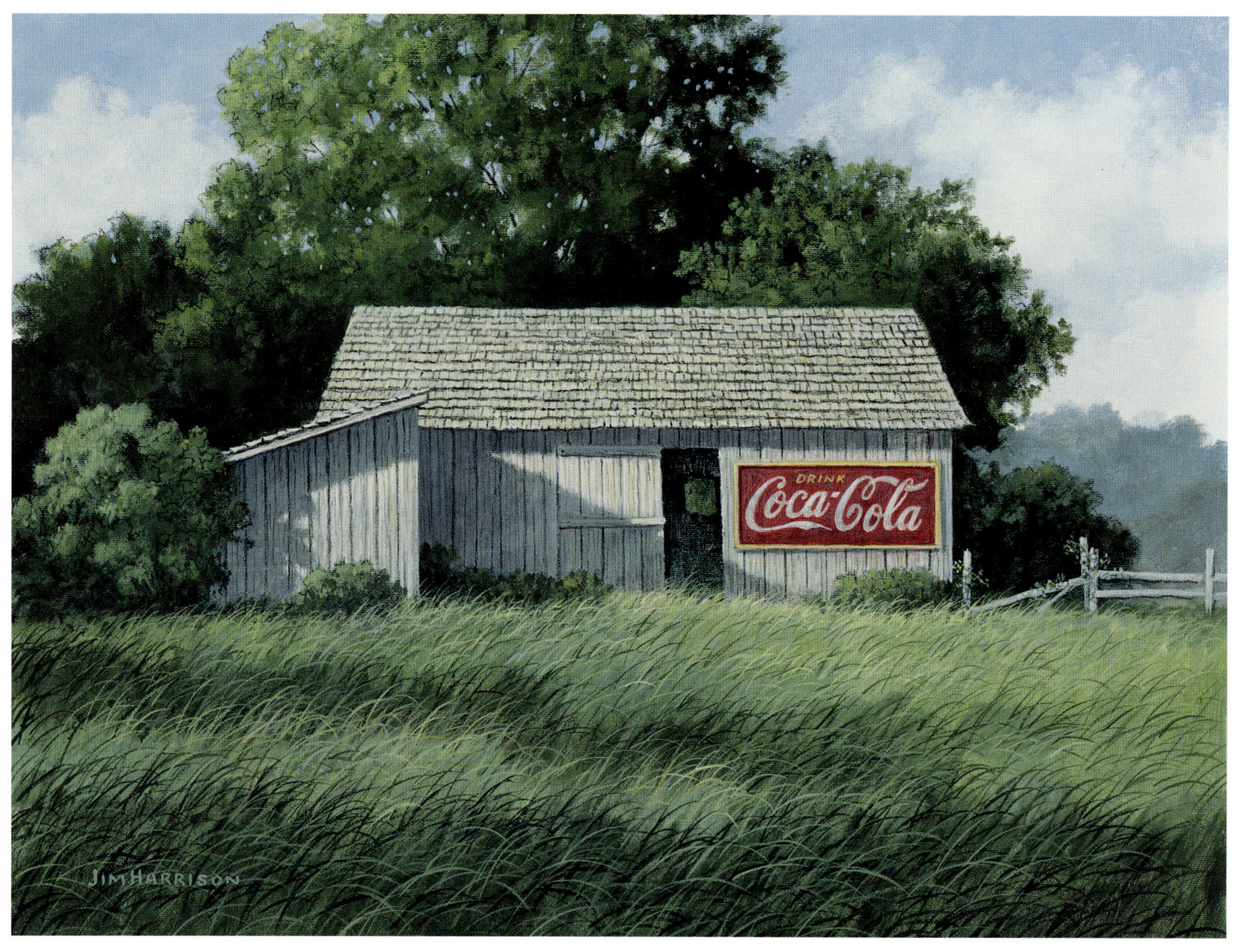


*June 2003*

ACRYLIC ON CANVAS, 14 × 18 INCHES, 2002

In hot weather Mr. Cornforth liked to work early in the cool mornings. The only problem with that was the dew, so we would spend some time waiting for the moisture to dry.

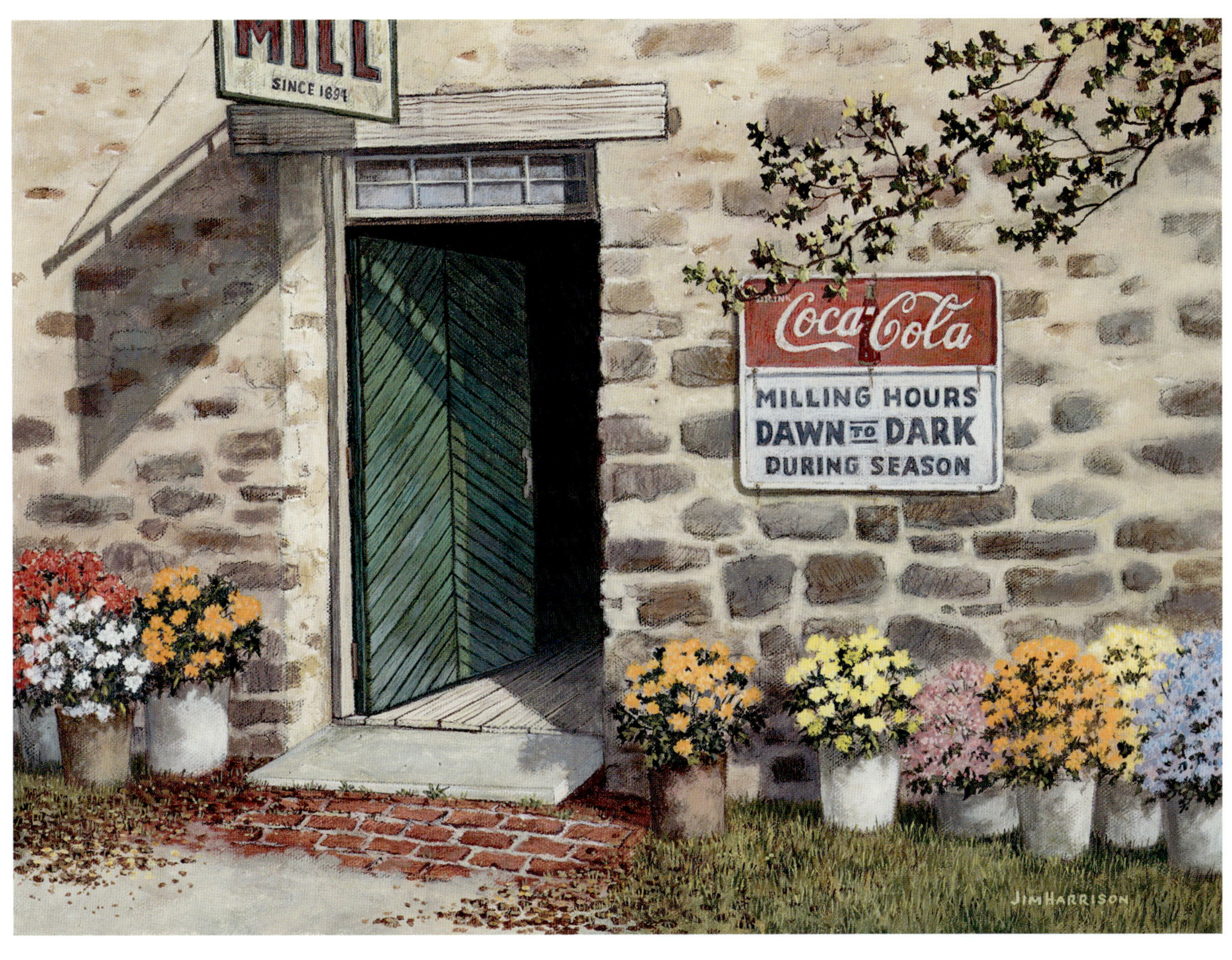


*May 2003*

ACRYLIC ON CANVAS, 12 × 16 INCHES, 1999

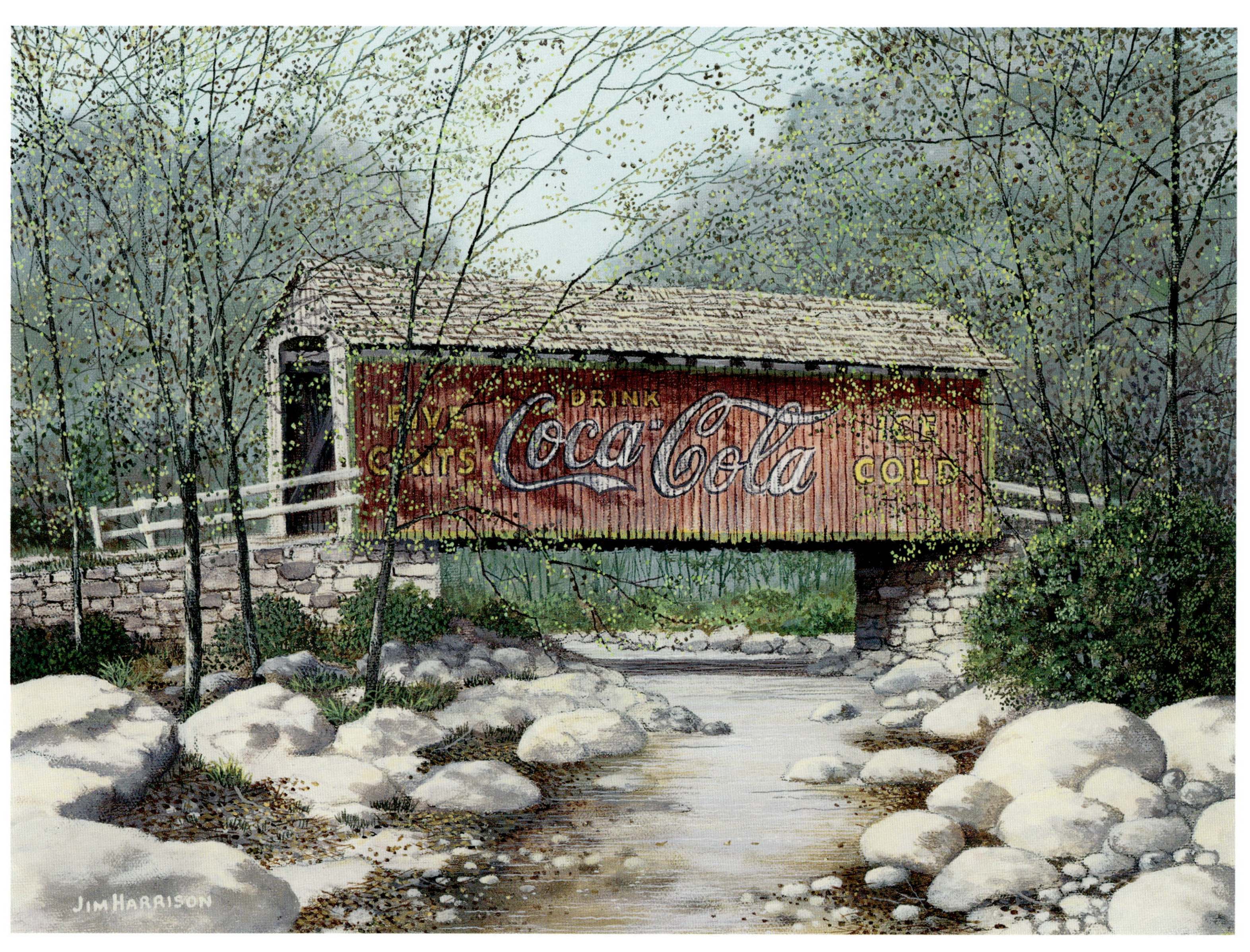


*April 2003*

ACRYLIC ON CANVAS, 12 × 16 INCHES, 1999

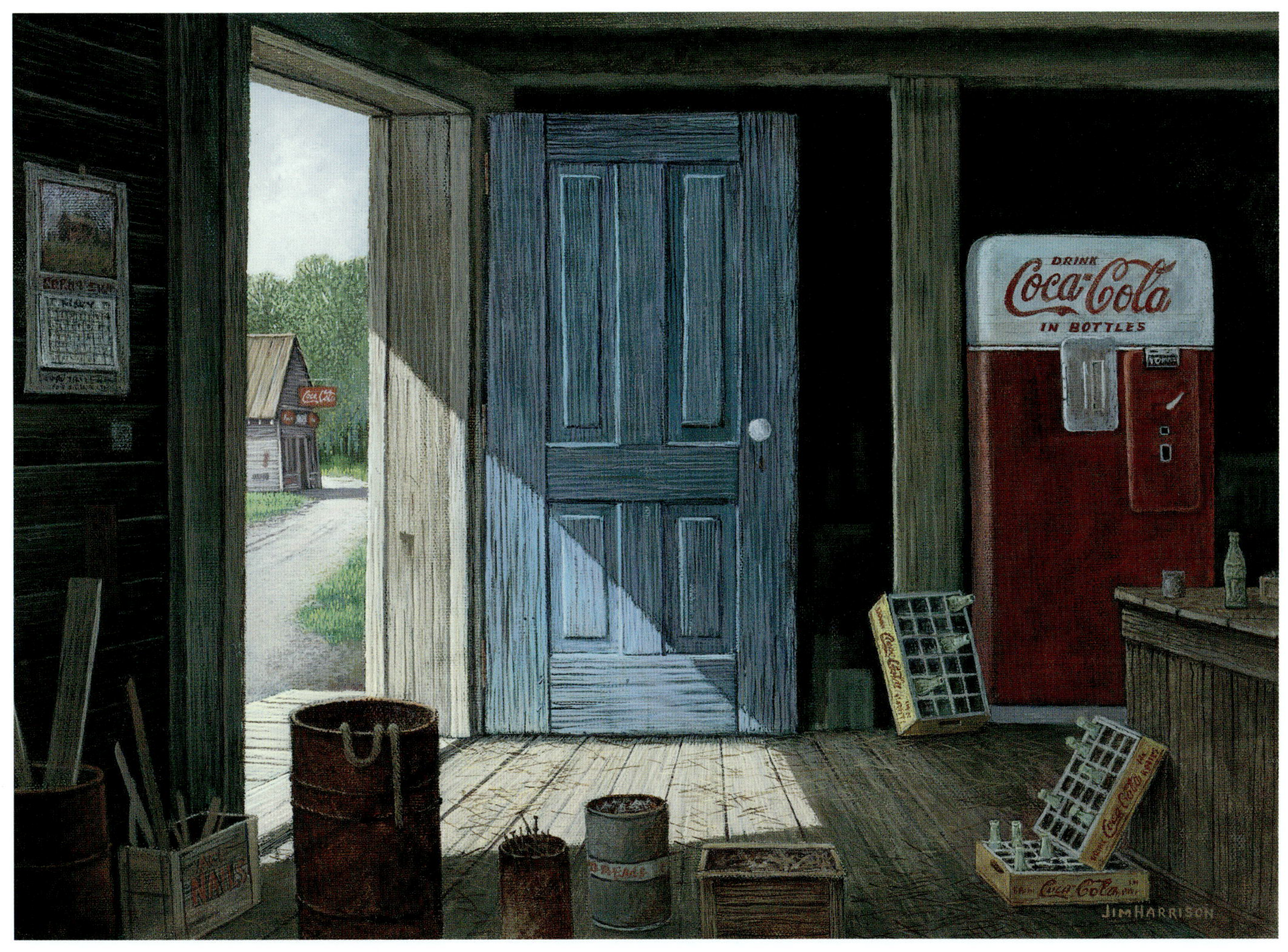


*The Old Store*

ACRYLIC ON CANVAS, 12.5 × 17 INCHES, 1999

In the light and shadow of an old country store, the old structure's past can be felt, smelled, savored, and learned from.

## *Nickel Coke*

ACRYLIC ON CANVAS, 18 × 14 INCHES, 1976

Memories certainly play a part in my work. I can vividly remember moments from the summer months of the early 1950s when I painted Coca-Cola signs on the walls of country stores. People can learn and know about places and things from books or photographs. That's gaining knowledge and facts. I'm talking about remembering, which is quite different. We remember with emotion what we experience. Most of my painting efforts have been an attempt to rekindle certain experiences of my past.

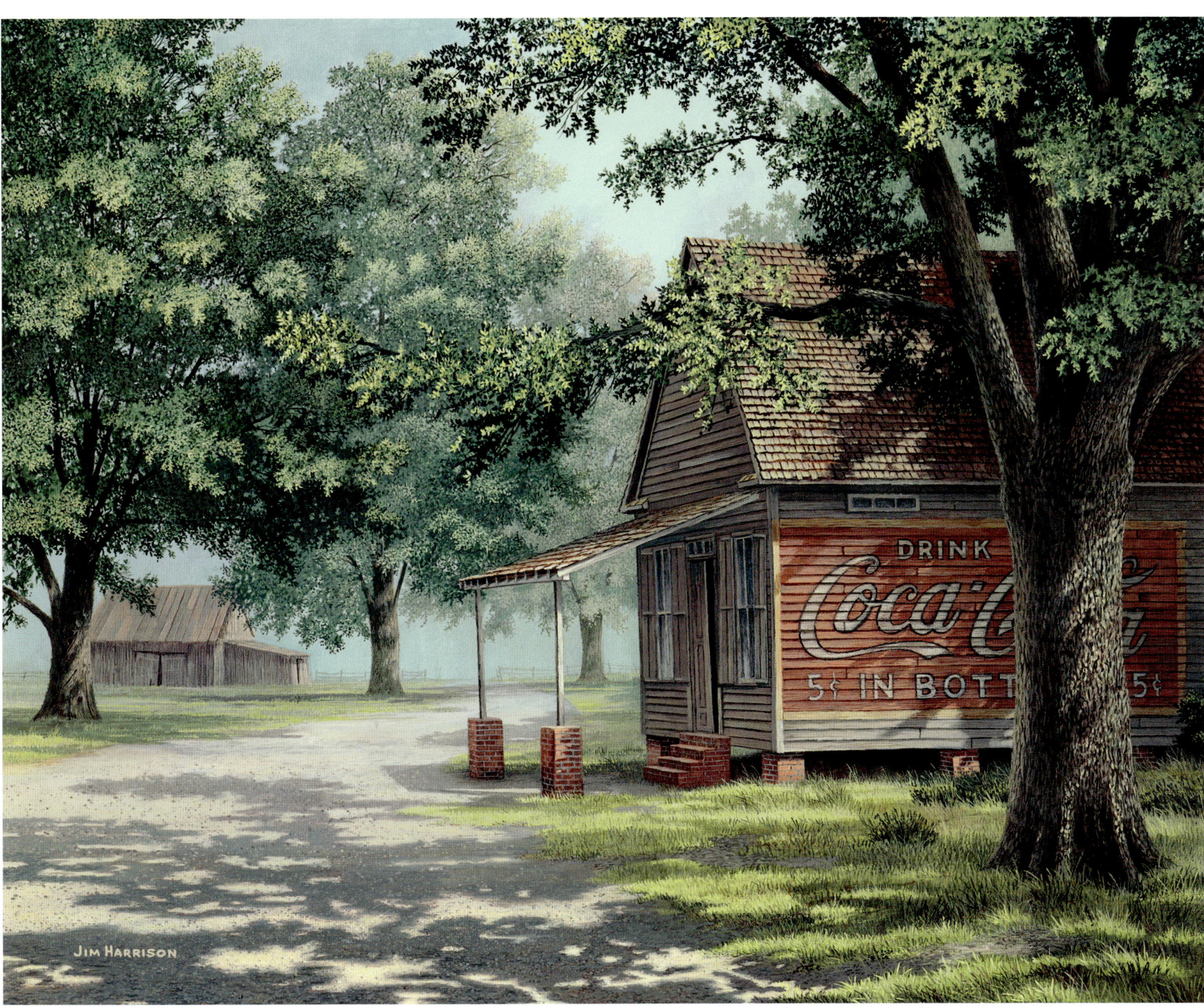
DRINK
JIM HARRISON

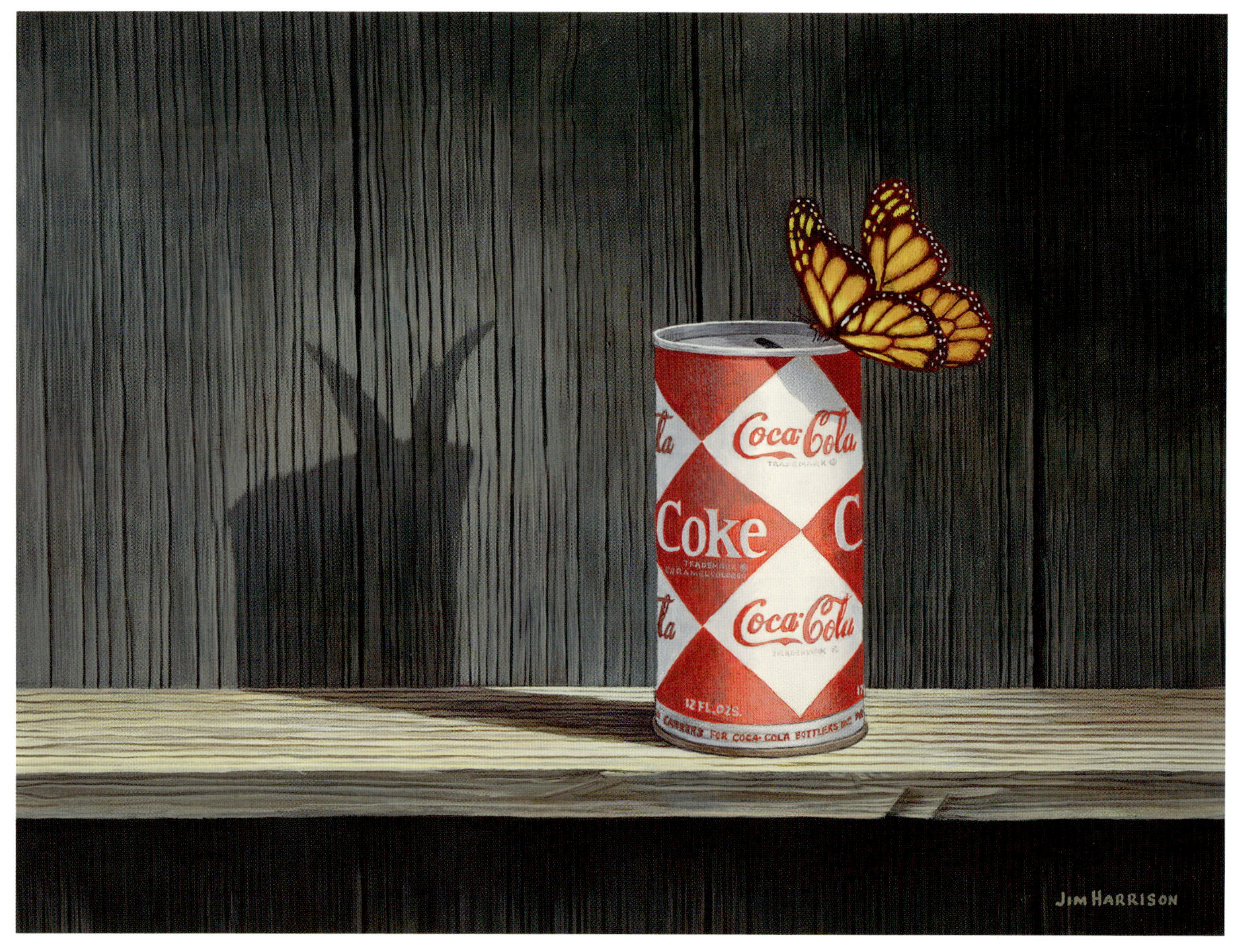


*Coke Can Butterfly*

ACRYLIC ON ILLUSTRATION BOARD, 11 × 14.5 INCHES, 1997

Nature and the passing of time have a way of taking the ugliness created by us and making it beautiful again.

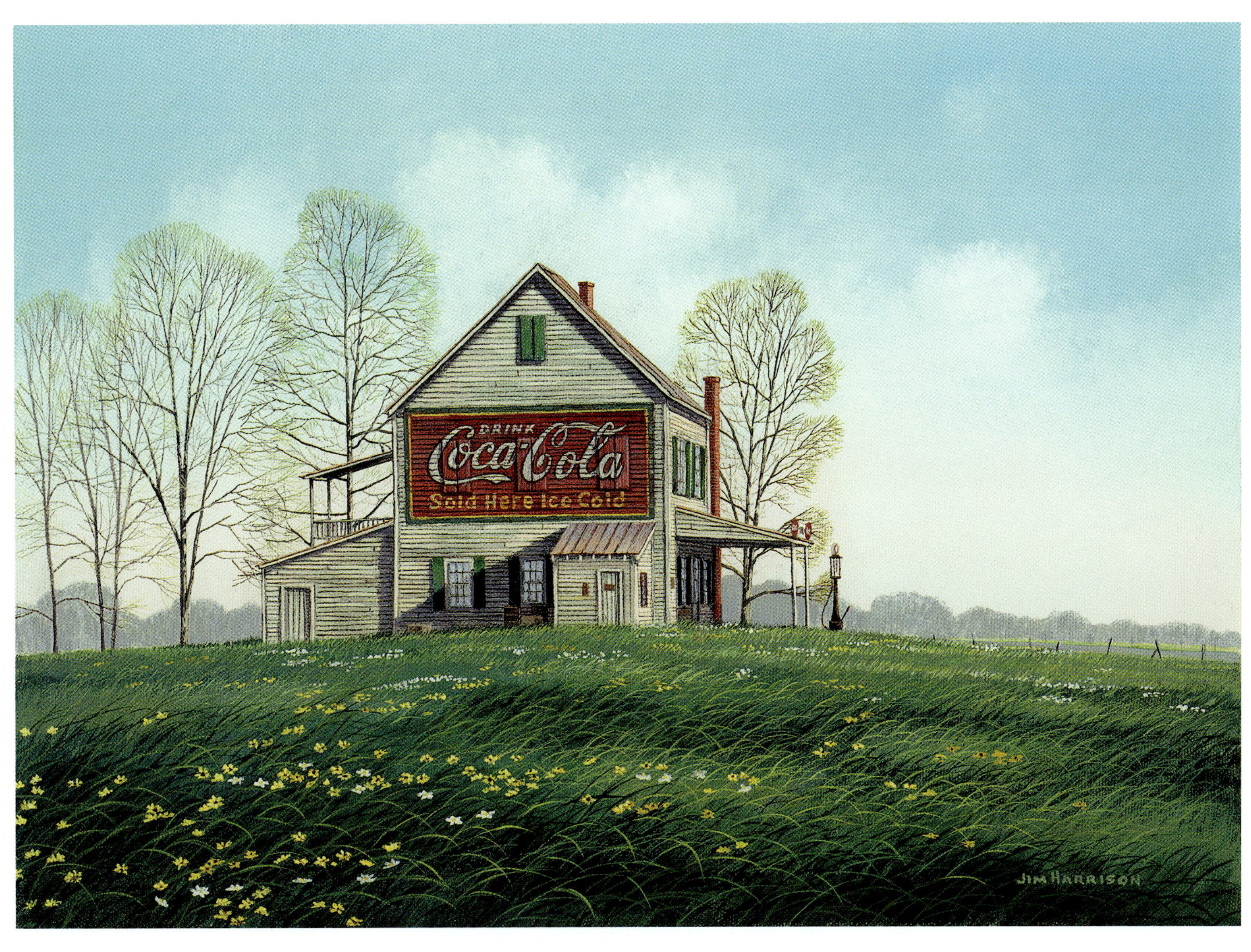


*Coca-Cola and Spring Flowers*

ACRYLIC ON ILLUSTRATION BOARD, 11 × 14.5 INCHES, 2010

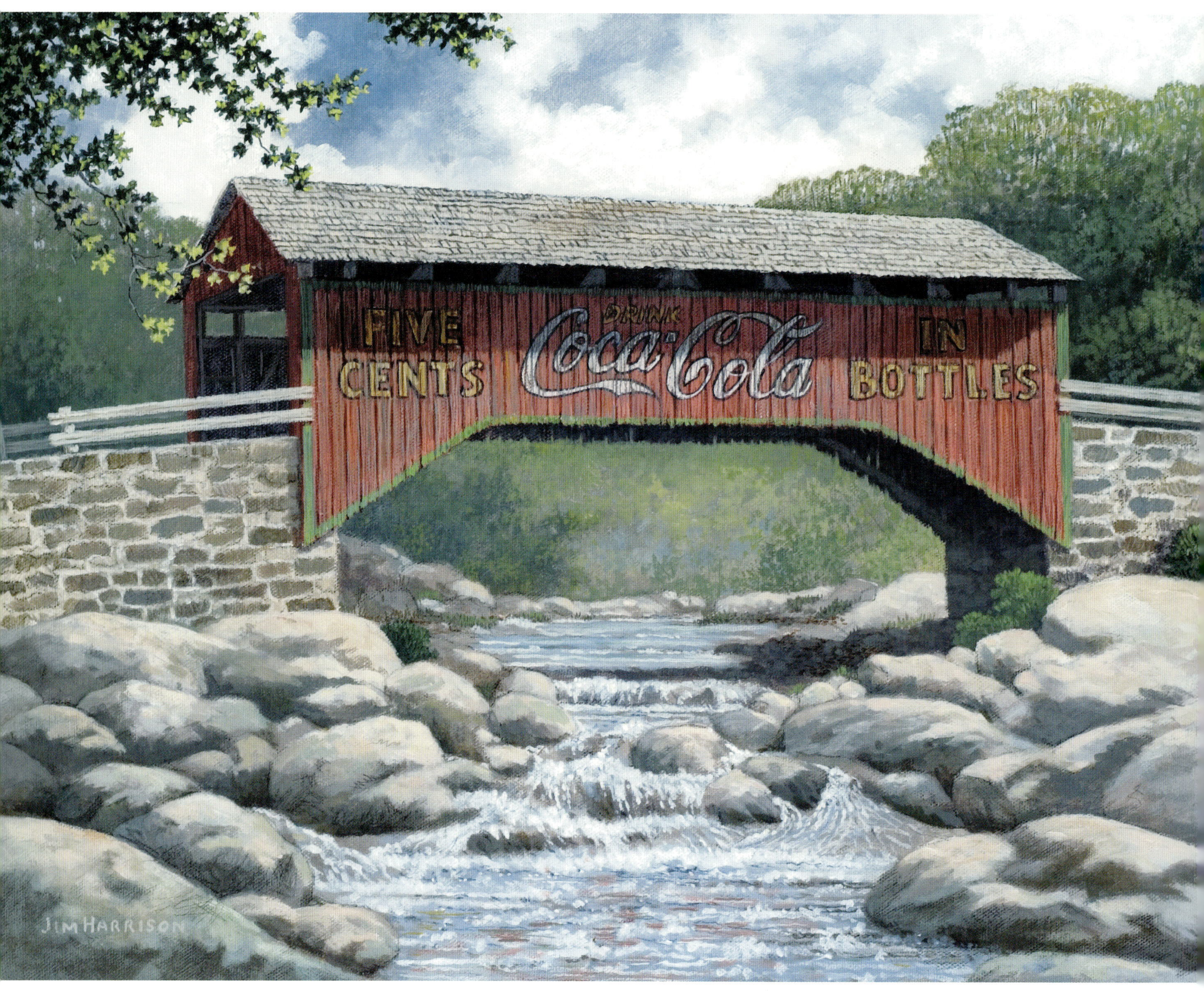
FIVE
CENTS
DRINK
Coca-Cola
IN
BOTTLES
JIM HARRISON

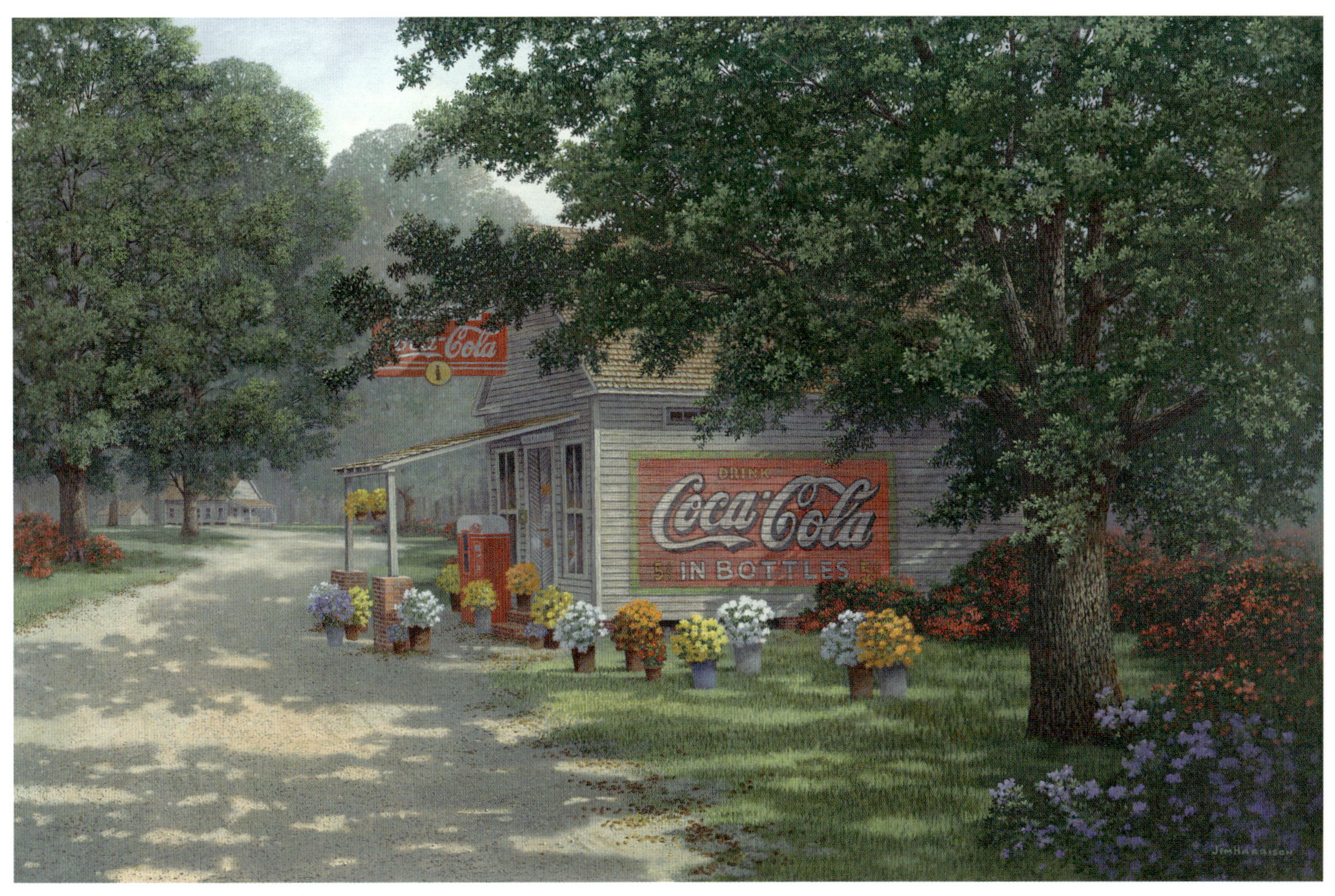


*Coca-Cola and Flowers*

ACRYLIC ON ILLUSTRATION BOARD, 11 × 14.5 INCHES, 2006

FACING *Coca-Cola Bridge and Rocky Creek*

ACRYLIC ON ILLUSTRATION BOARD, 11 × 14.5 INCHES, 2005

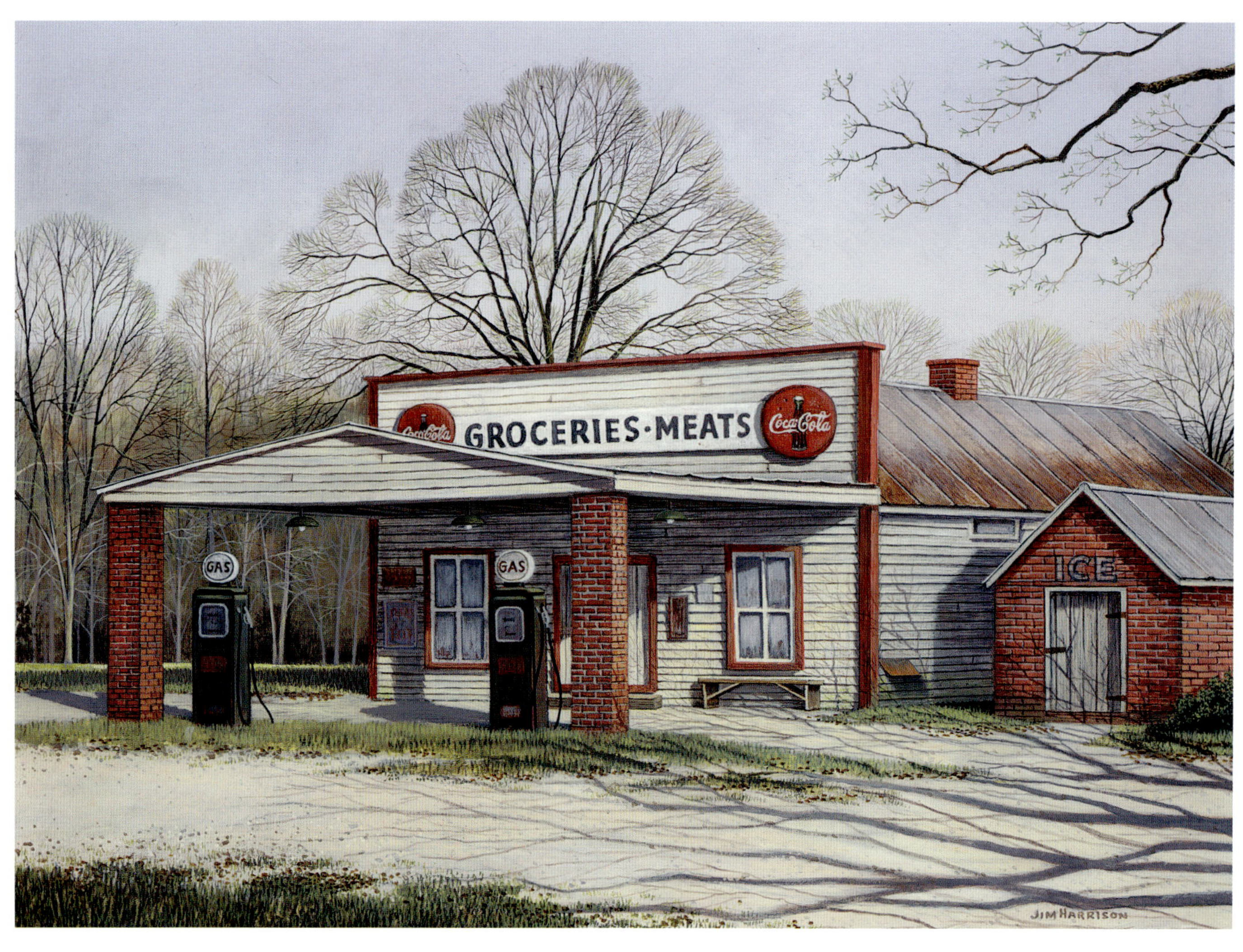


*Coca-Cola Groceries and Meats*

ACRYLIC ON ILLUSTRATION BOARD, 11 × 14.5 INCHES, 2010

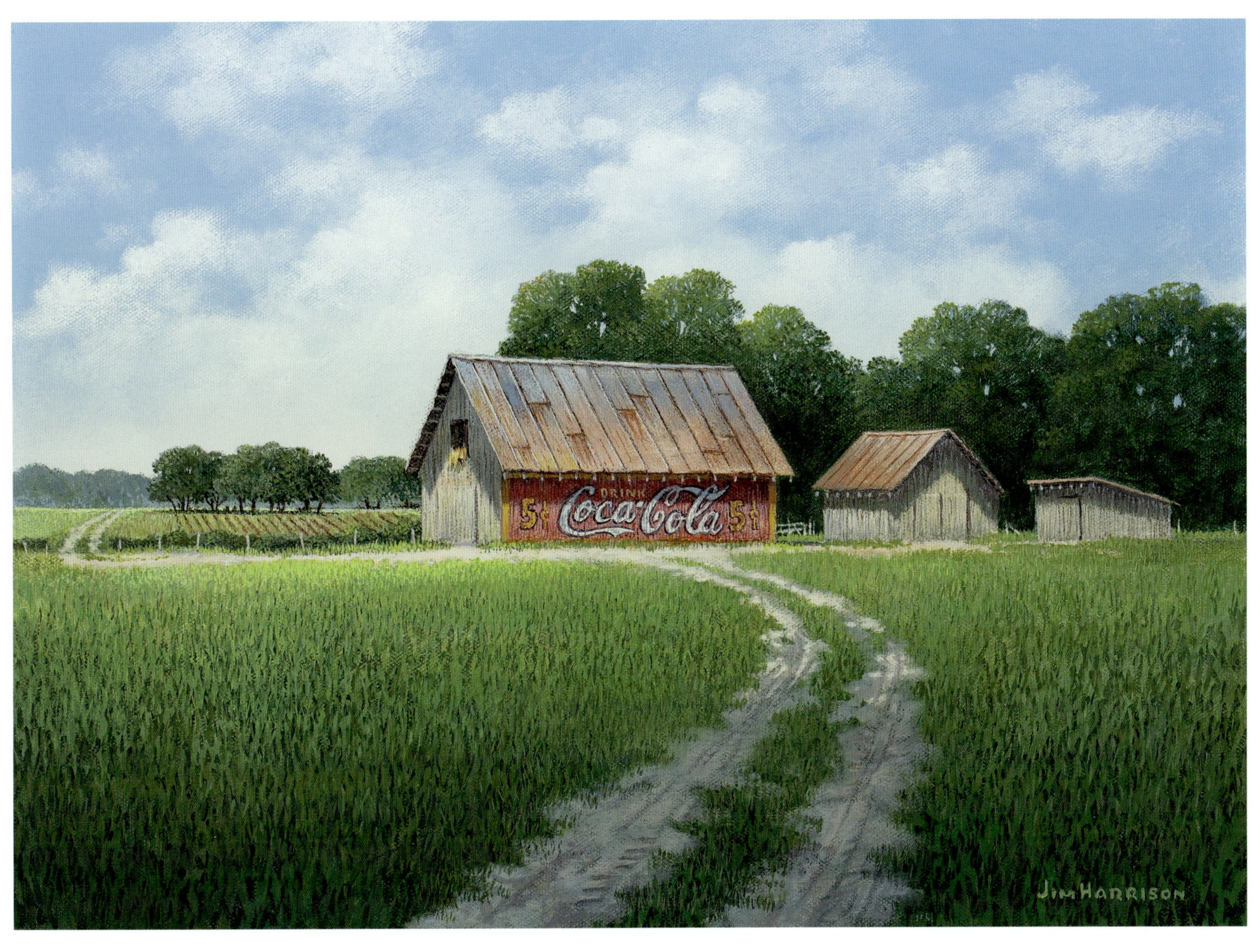


*Road to Coca-Cola Barn*

ACRYLIC ON ILLUSTRATION BOARD, 11 × 14.5 INCHES, 1997

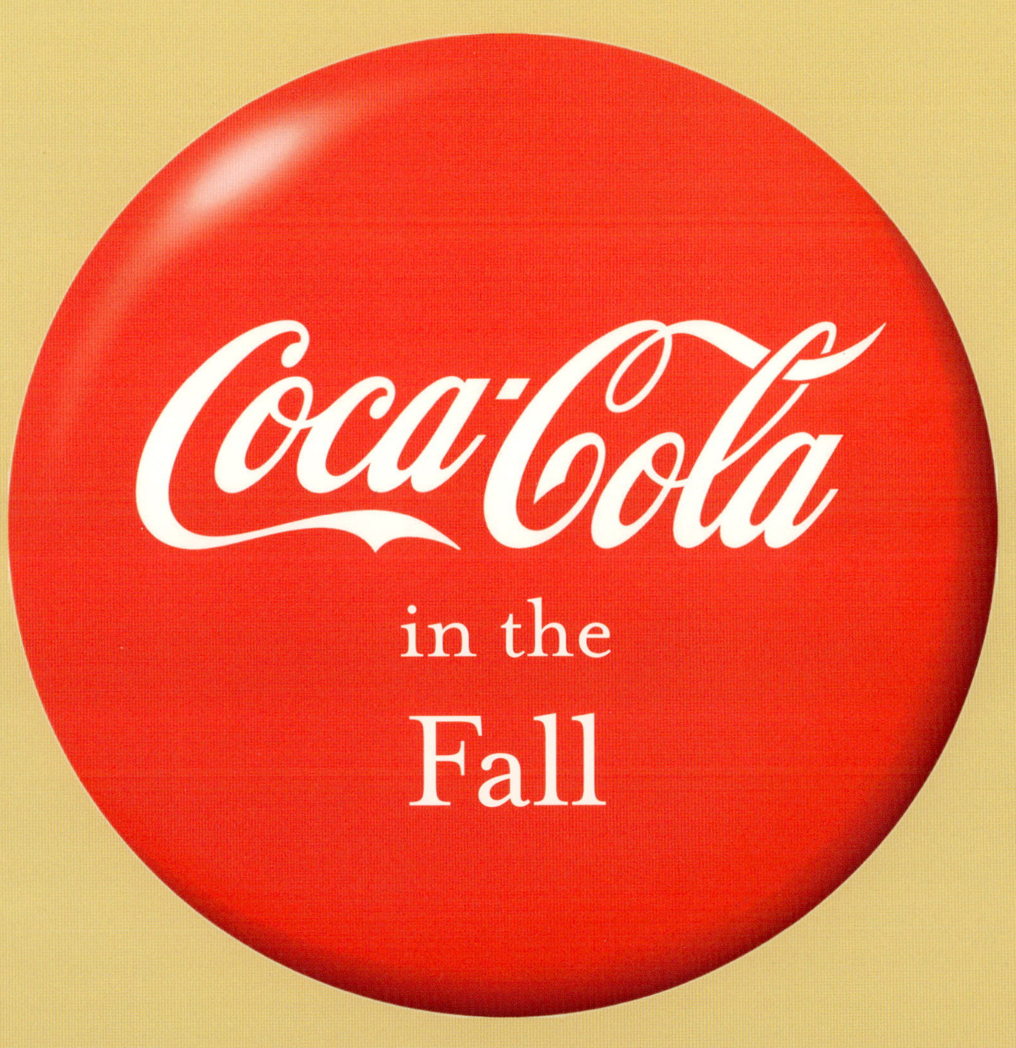
Coca-Cola
in the
Fall

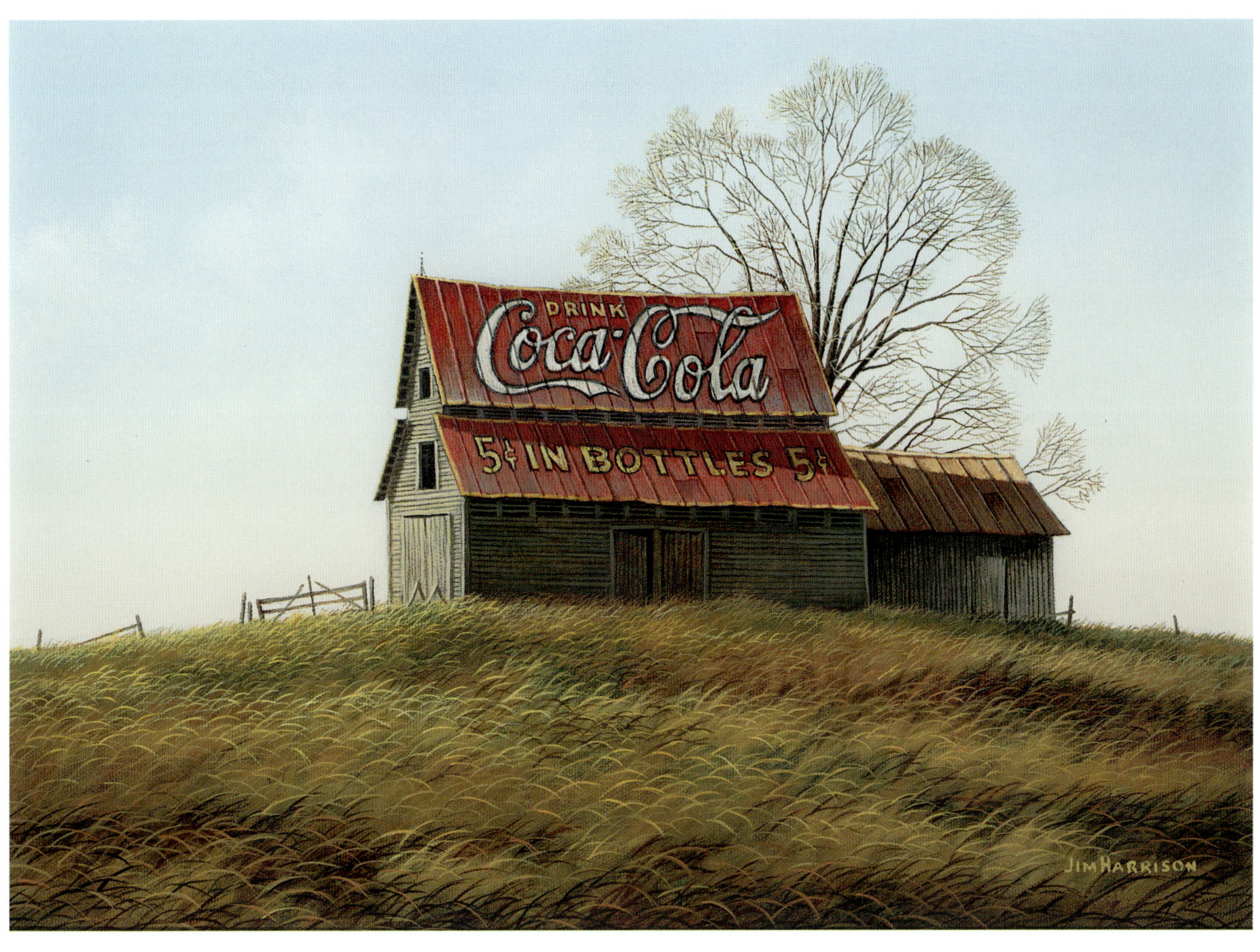


*Coca-Cola on the Hill*

ACRYLIC ON CANVAS, 12 × 16 INCHES, 1997

Painting a tin roof sign is tough. We did not paint a Coca-Cola sign on a roof, but we did some motel signs on them. A steeply pitched roof was impossible to stand on. We had to rig ladders with ropes to remain steady.

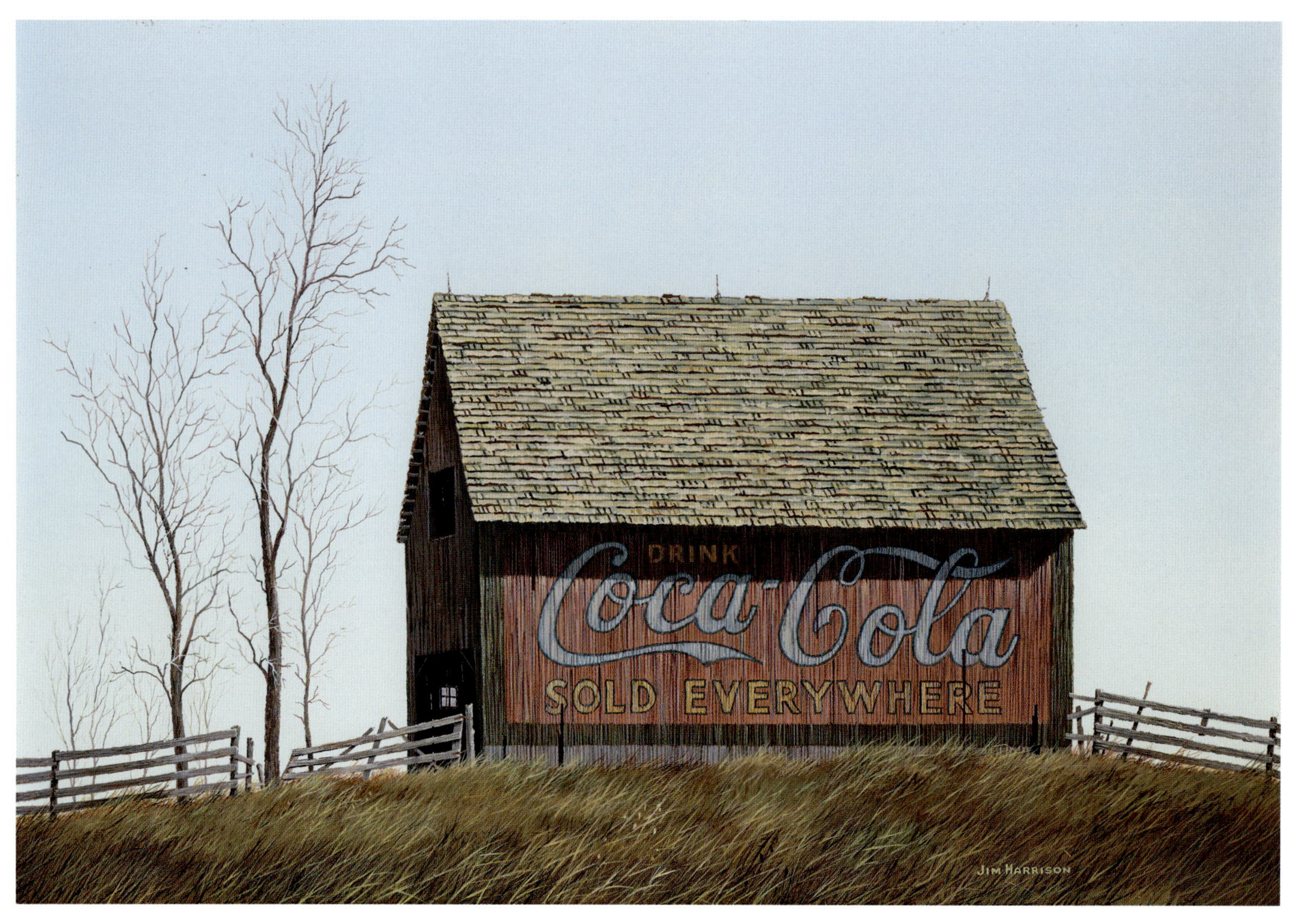


*Coca-Cola Barn*

ACRYLIC ON MASONITE, 14 × 18 INCHES, 2001

I never really saw myself as a sign painter the rest of my life. I didn't see myself becoming a full-time artist either. The twists and turns of life are always interesting in retrospect.

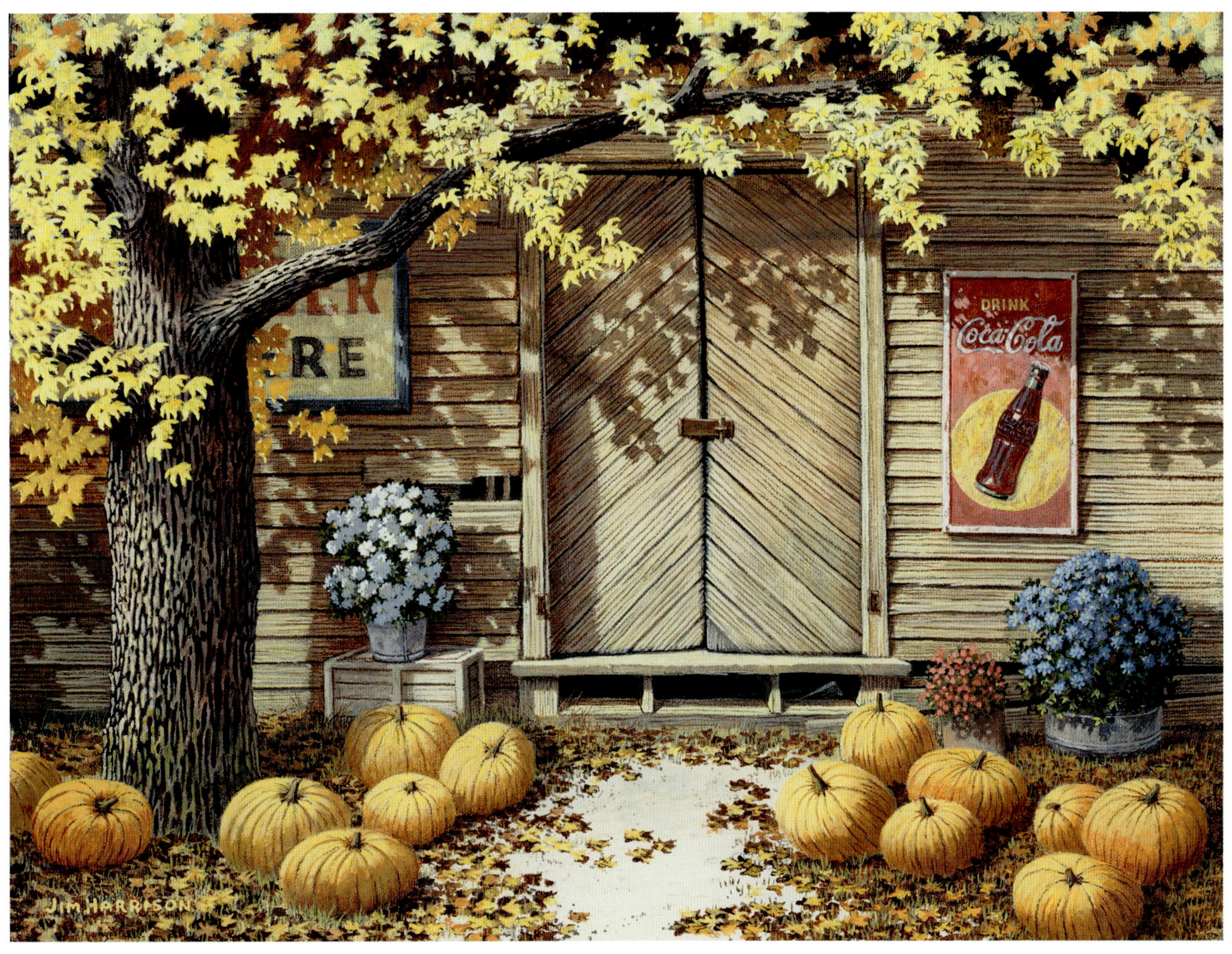


*Coca-Cola Fall Pumpkins*

ACRYLIC ON CANVAS, 14 × 18 INCHES, 1996

Mr. Cornforth was quite a gentleman, and he always tipped his hat to ladies as we met them on the street.

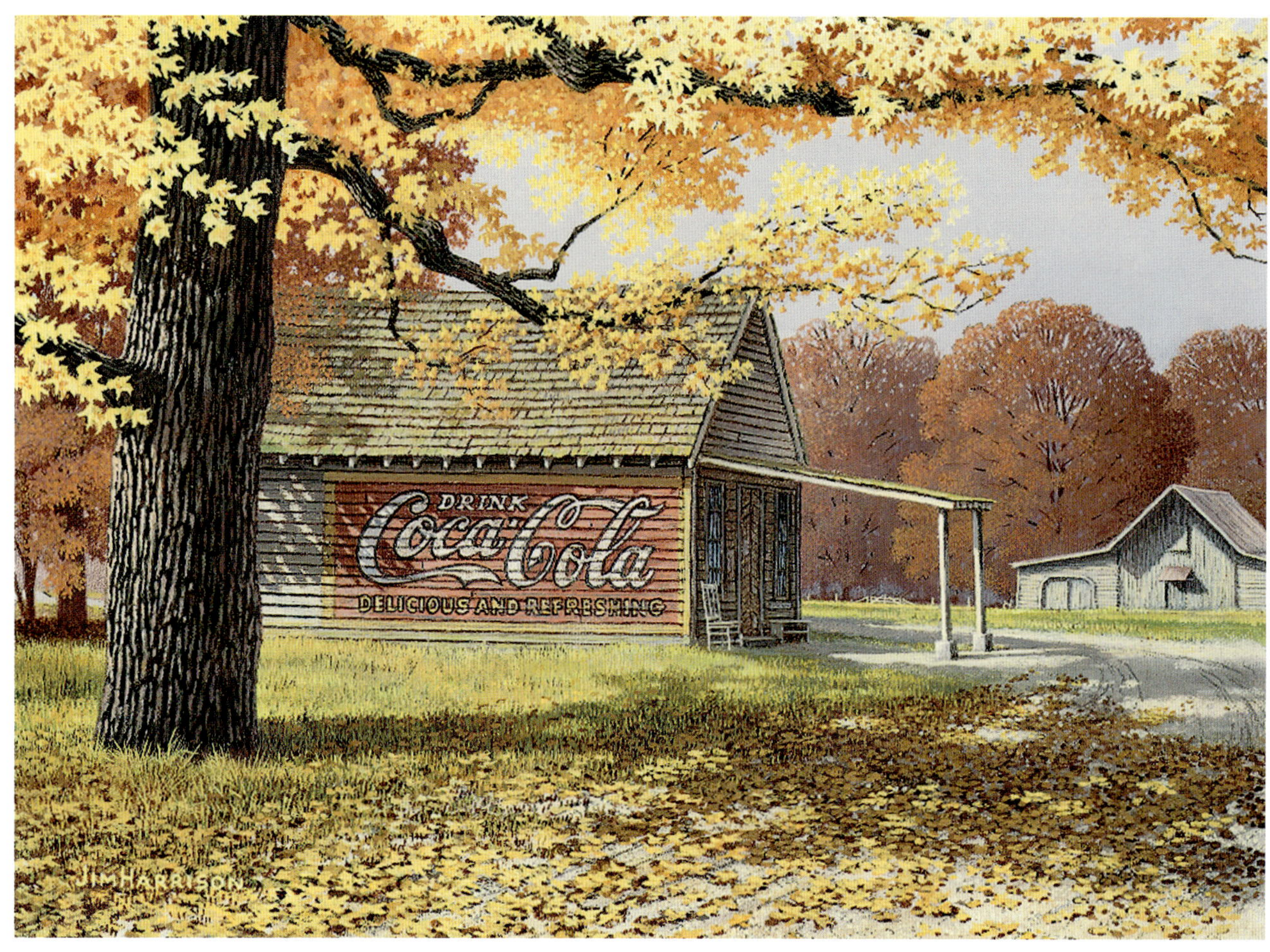


*Coca-Cola in September*

ACRYLIC ON CANVAS, 12 × 16 INCHES, 1996

My many years with Coke have taken different gentle circular turns. I didn't recognize this until just the other day, when I found myself looking back while sitting in almost the same spot where I started with Mr. Cornforth over half a century ago.

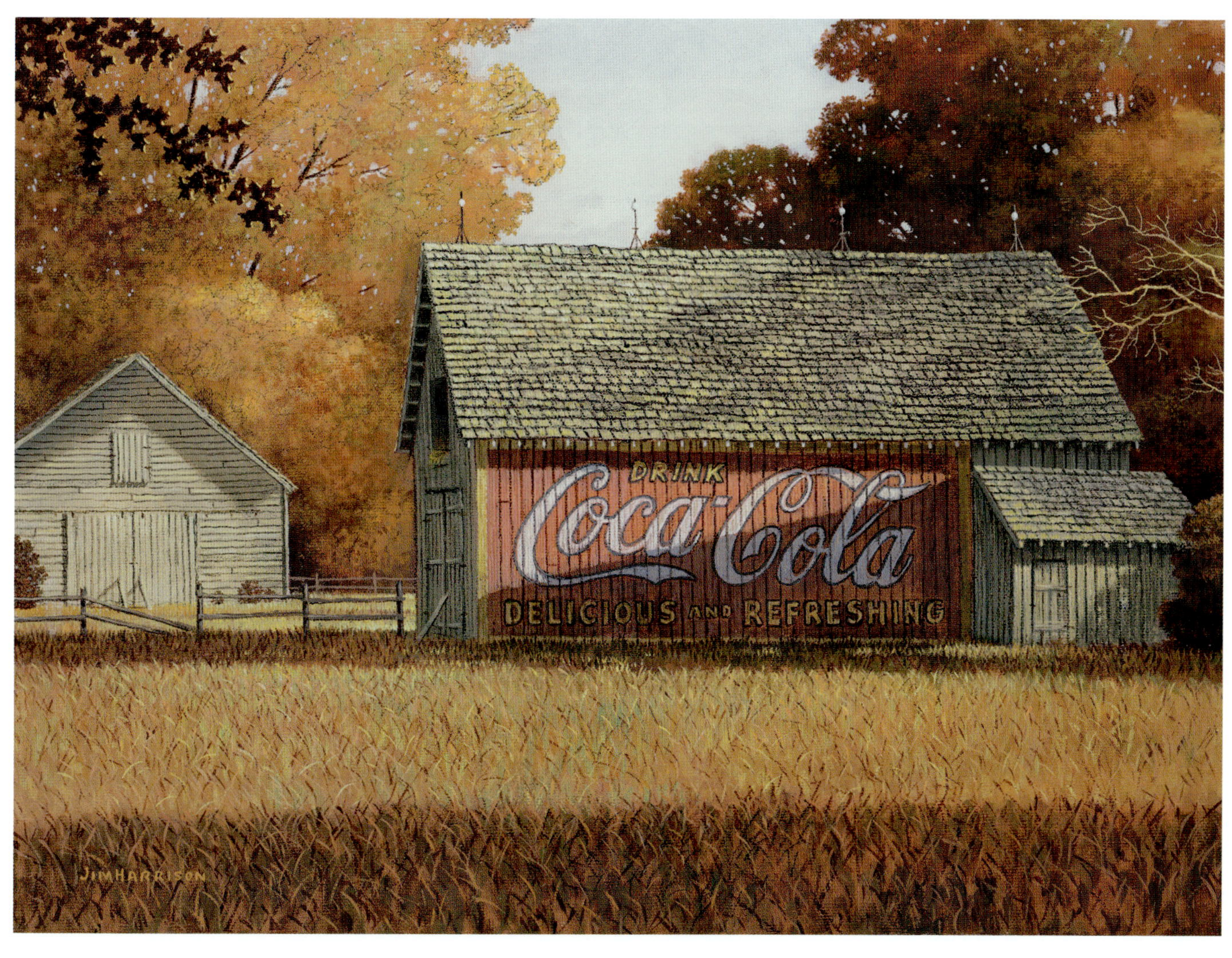


*Coca-Cola in October*

ACRYLIC ON CANVAS, 13 × 17 INCHES, 2001

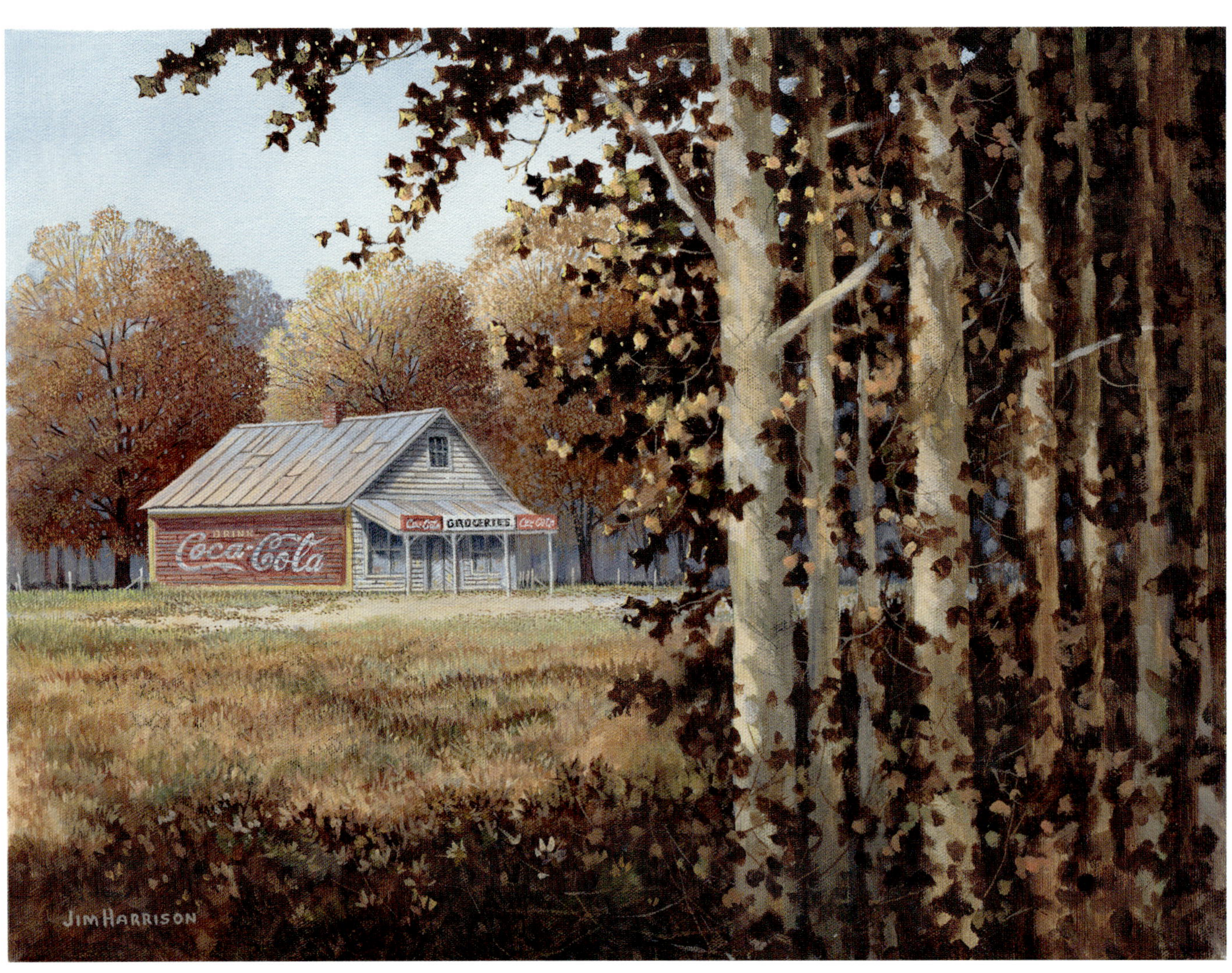
DRINK
Coca-Cola
GROCERIES
JIM HARRISON

*Coca-Cola September 2002*

ACRYLIC ON CANVAS, 14 × 18 INCHES, 2002

The experiences I got with Mr. Cornforth were encouraging. We made a good team. He told me that anybody could learn to do this with practice, and it gave me confidence. I became precise in making letters, and I wouldn't hesitate to paint on the side of a school bus. That required good lettering—exact. But my greatest enjoyment came from the work I would do with Mr. Cornforth on large outdoor bulletins, often on the sides of country stores in the remote rural areas of Denmark. In the fall of one year, as the weather became cooler, we repainted almost a dozen of the large signs for the Coca-Cola Company.

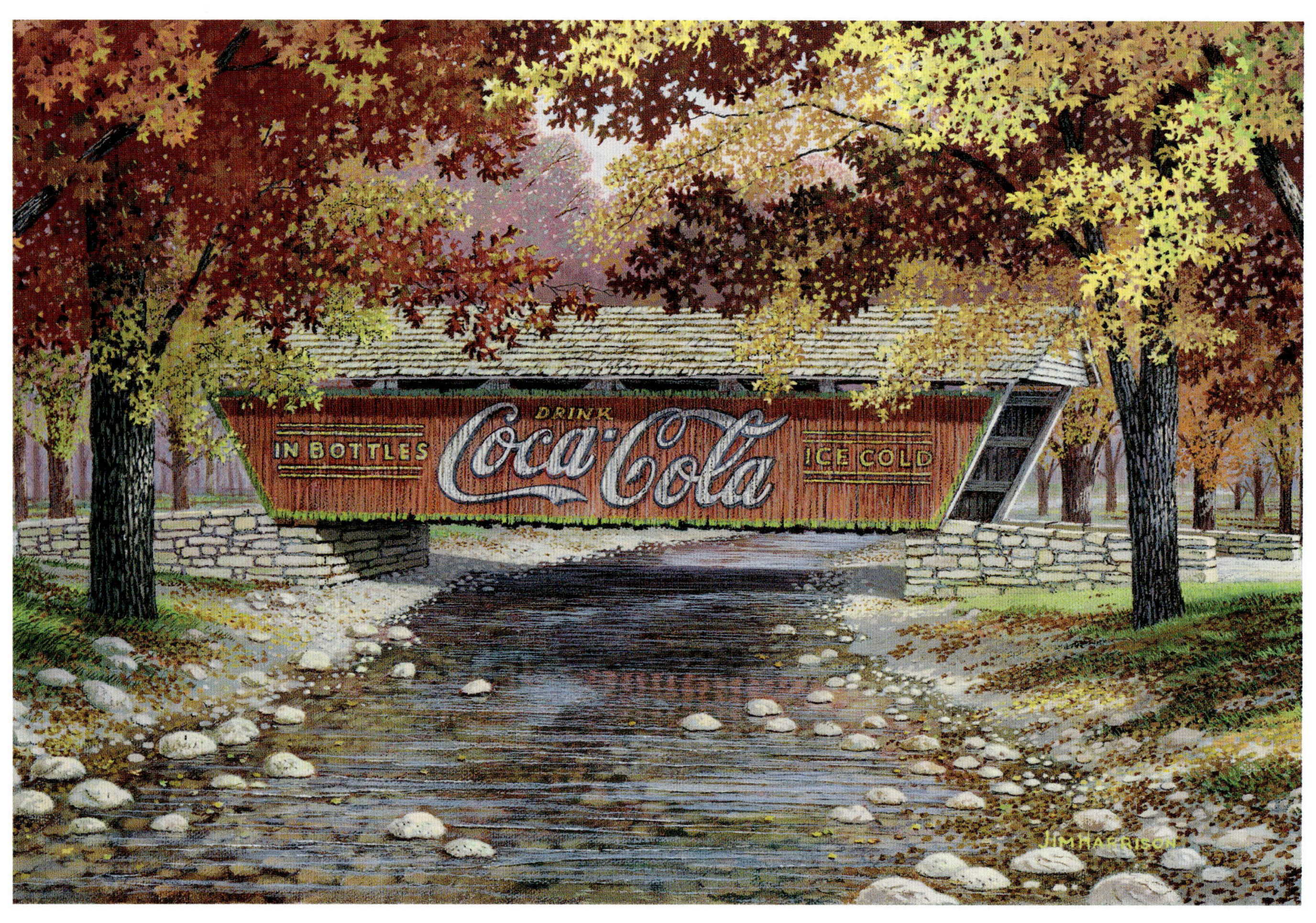


*Coca-Cola Covered Bridge in September*

ACRYLIC ON CANVAS, 12 × 24 INCHES, 1997

Coca-Cola quickly crossed all social, racial, and economic lines. It was the same to everyone. A Coke was a Coke, and the cold, refreshing enjoyment could be purchased by anyone with a nickel. According to a 1920 survey, Coca-Cola sales accounted for more transactions at country stores than any other single item. It has become a permanent part of the American scene.

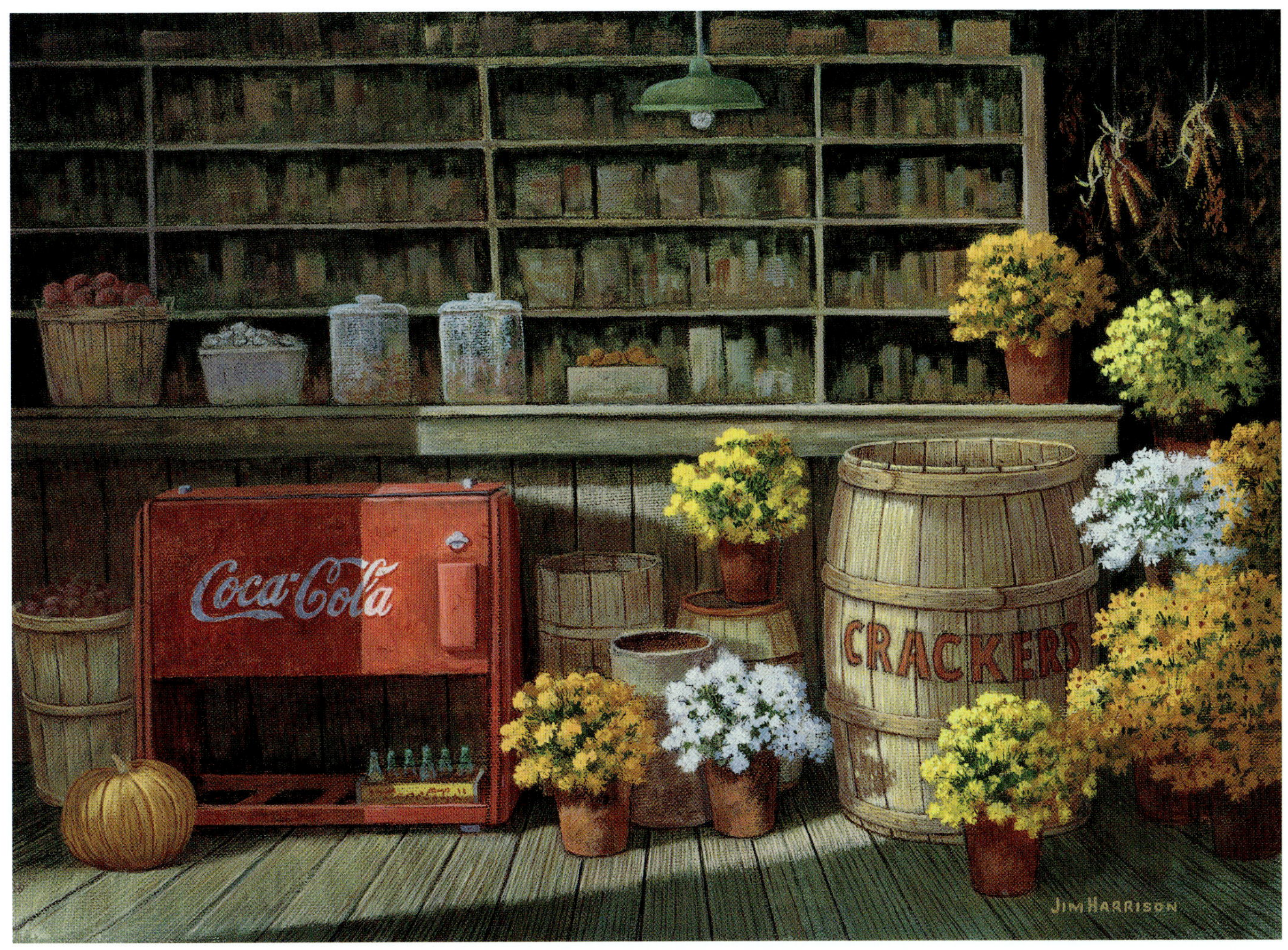


*Country Store in Fall*

ACRYLIC ON CANVAS, 12 × 16 INCHES, 2000

I liked the challenge of leaving early in the morning to work all day scraping and repainting the huge signs, some of which were fifteen feet tall and perhaps thirty feet long. These were the times which whetted my appetite for the sign painter's craft. At lunch we'd stop and go into the store and get a big Pepsi Cola—even though we might

CONTINUED NEXT PAGE

be painting a Coca-Cola sign—and sweet rolls, some cheese, and some bologna. And that would be our lunch. And it was mighty good. Even to this day, I enjoy going out to a country store and getting that kind of stuff. I can make a meal out of it, and a pretty good meal, at that.

## *Fall, Flowers, and Coca-Cola*

ACRYLIC ON CANVAS, 12 × 16 INCHES, 1996

For almost a century "ice-cold Coca-Cola" has been hawked around the world at sporting events, movie houses, political rallies, and any other conceivable public gathering. Born in a boiling black pot in the backyard of a two-story, red-brick building in Atlanta, Georgia, the universal thirst-quencher has become the world's best-known American product. It has been claimed that the Coca-Cola trademark can be seen in any direction from any street corner in the world. In its quest to be the most recognizable trademark, Coca-Cola through its advertising has poured, refreshed, invigorated, and enjoyed its way into the hearts of hot and thirsty people all over the world.

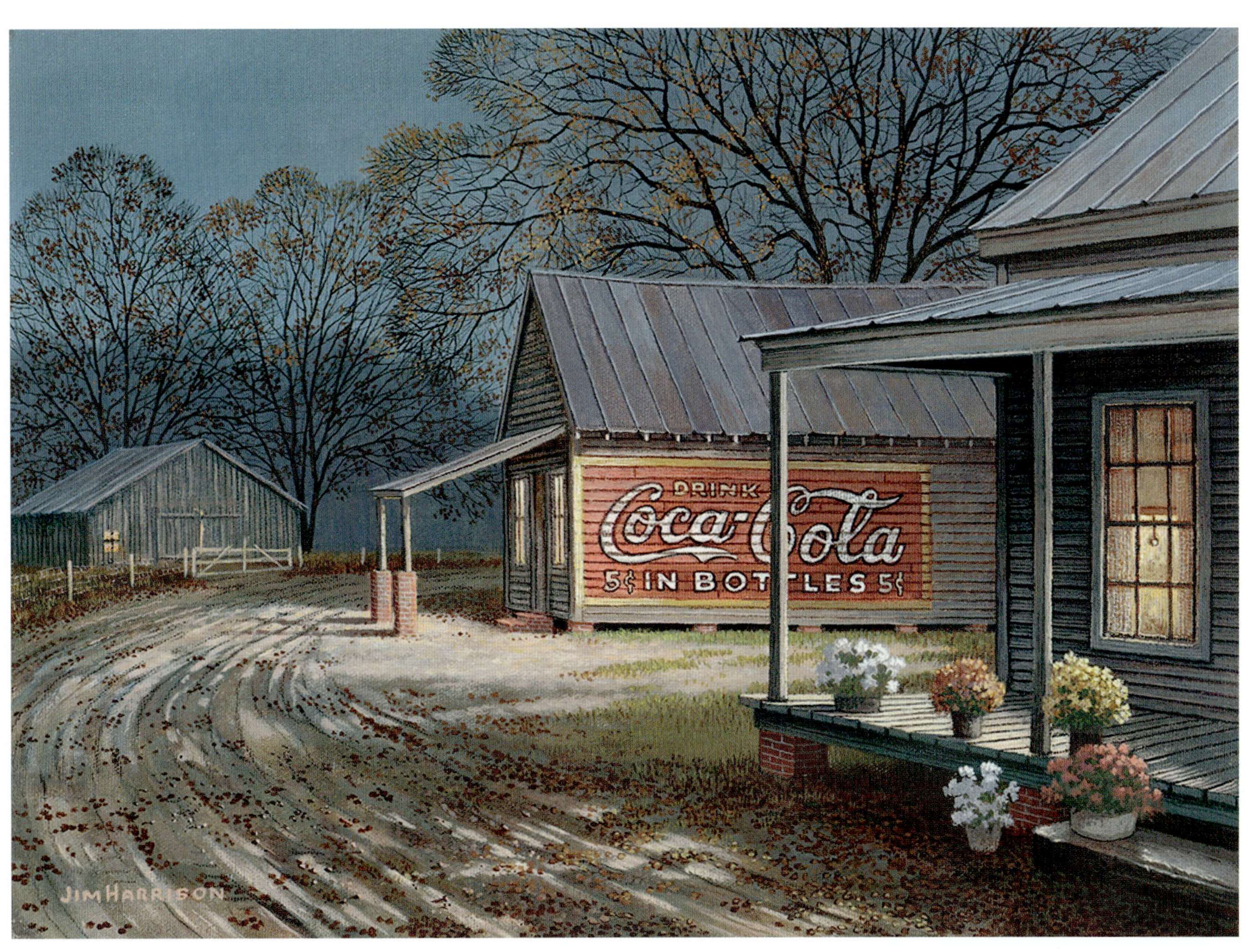
DRINK
Coca-Cola
5¢ IN BOTTLES 5¢
JIM HARRISON

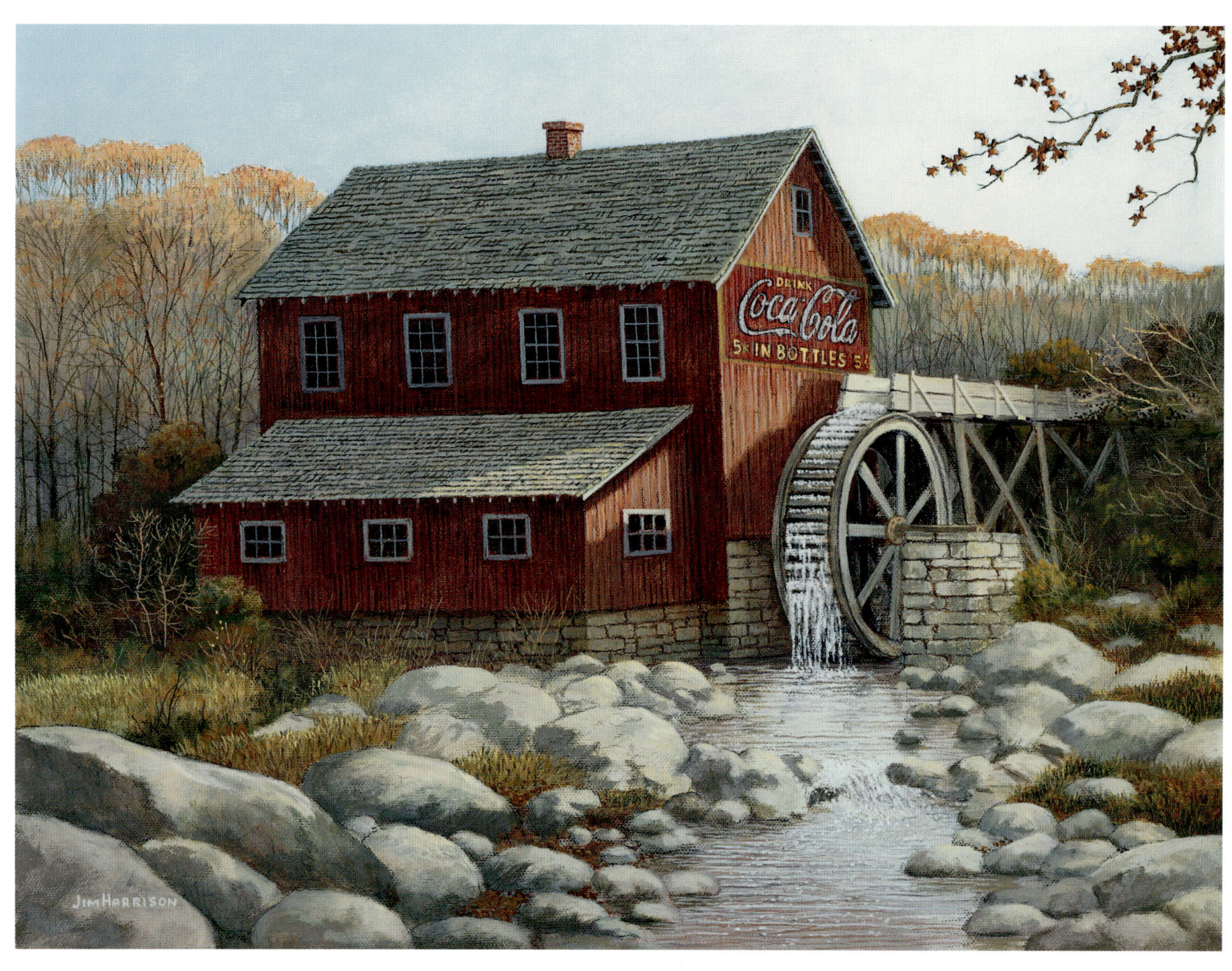


*November 2000*

ACRYLIC ON CANVAS, 14 × 18 INCHES, 1999

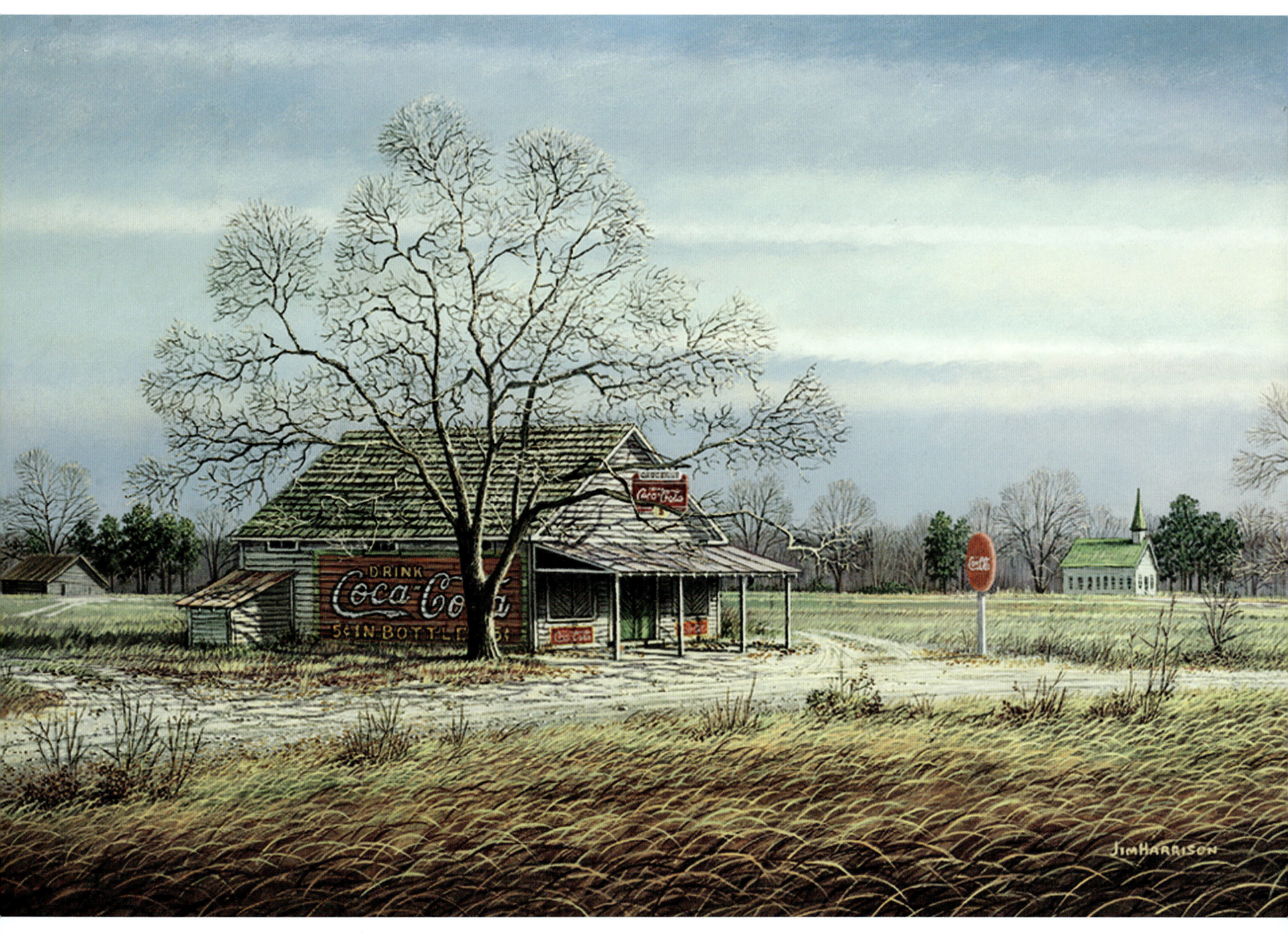


*November 2001*

ACRYLIC ON CANVAS, 15 × 30 INCHES, 1998

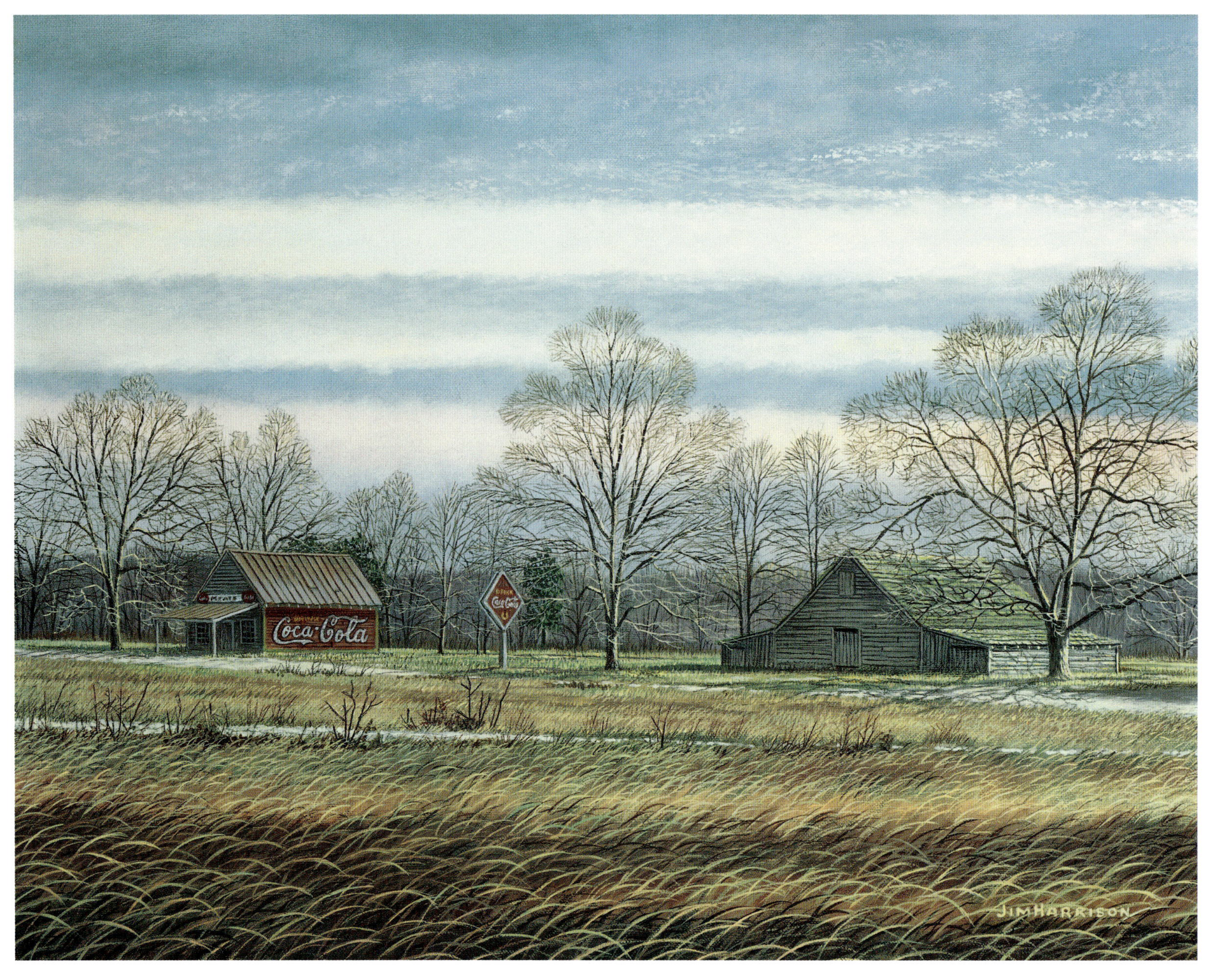


*November 2003*

ACRYLIC ON CANVAS, 15 × 30 INCHES, 1998

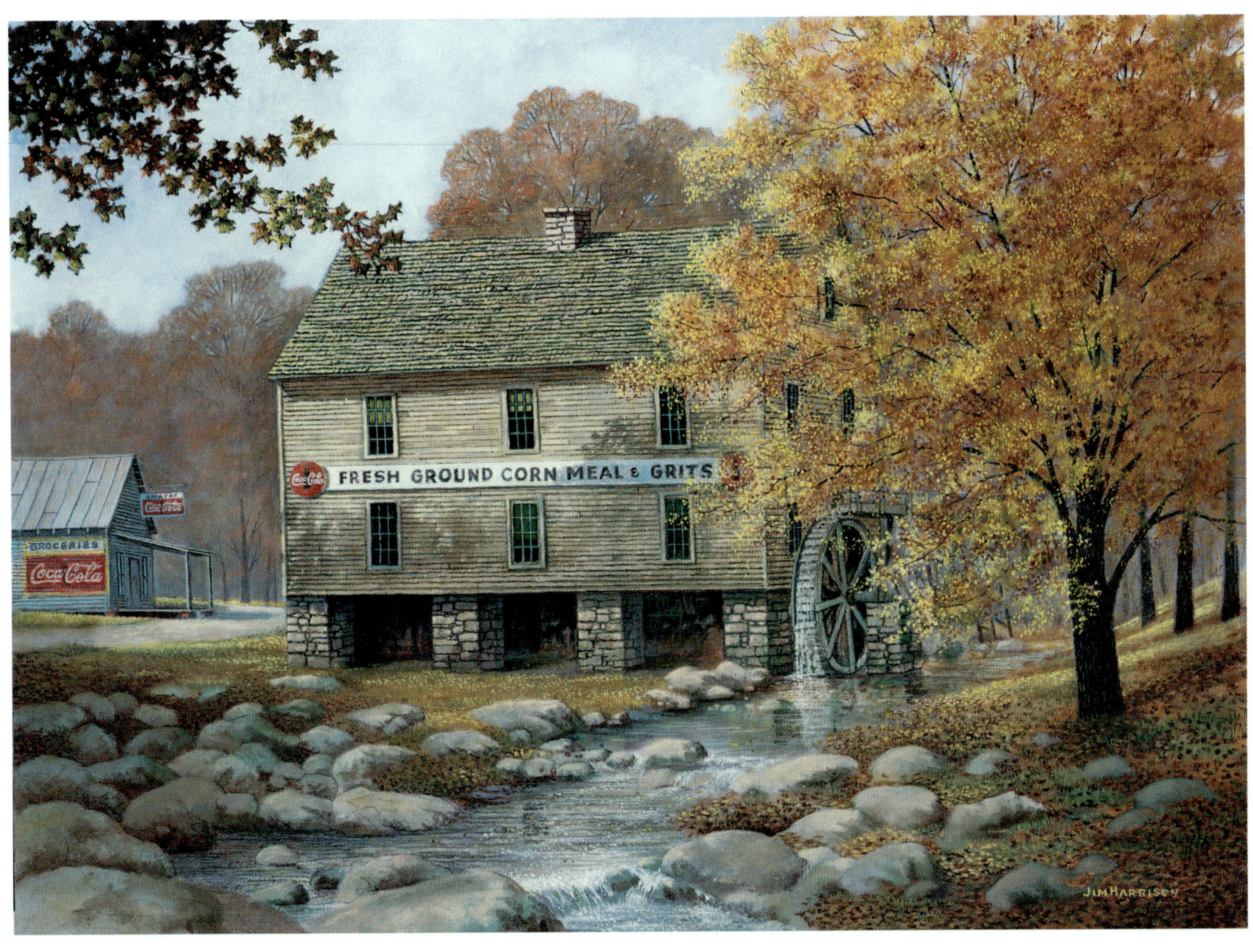


*October 2000*

ACRYLIC ON CANVAS, 18 × 24 INCHES, 1999

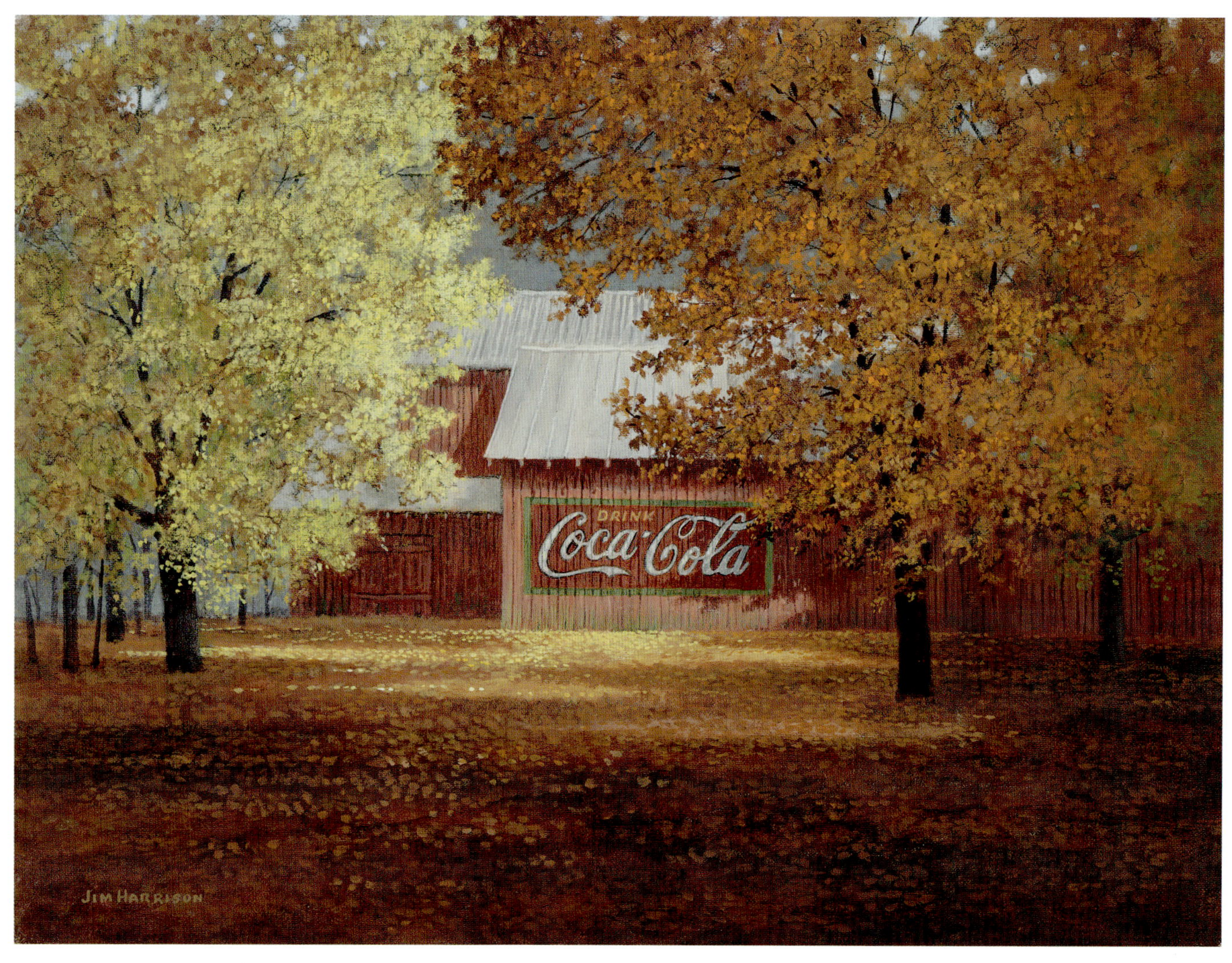


*October 2003*

ACRYLIC ON CANVAS, 14 × 18 INCHES, 2002

I do attach certain feelings and emotions to seasons and to seasonal pictures. Anything fall means football to me. I reserve all fall Saturdays for me and football games.

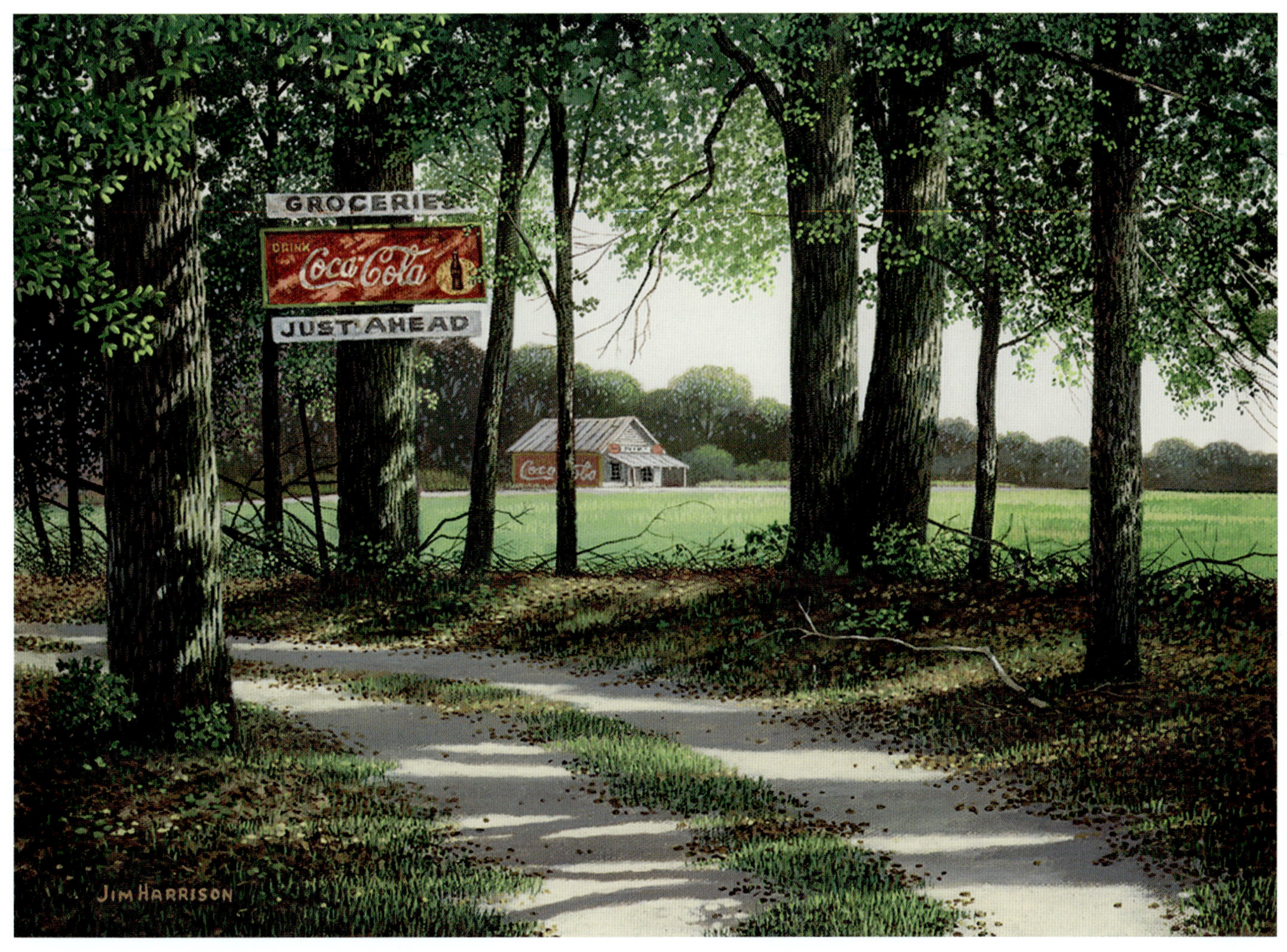


*September 2001*

ACRYLIC ON CANVAS, 12 × 16 INCHES, 1998

Some of my best compositions include a small road curving through the woods, leading to a building of some sort in the distance, with shadows breaking across the sandy ruts and some fallen, colorful leaves; fall always appeals to me.

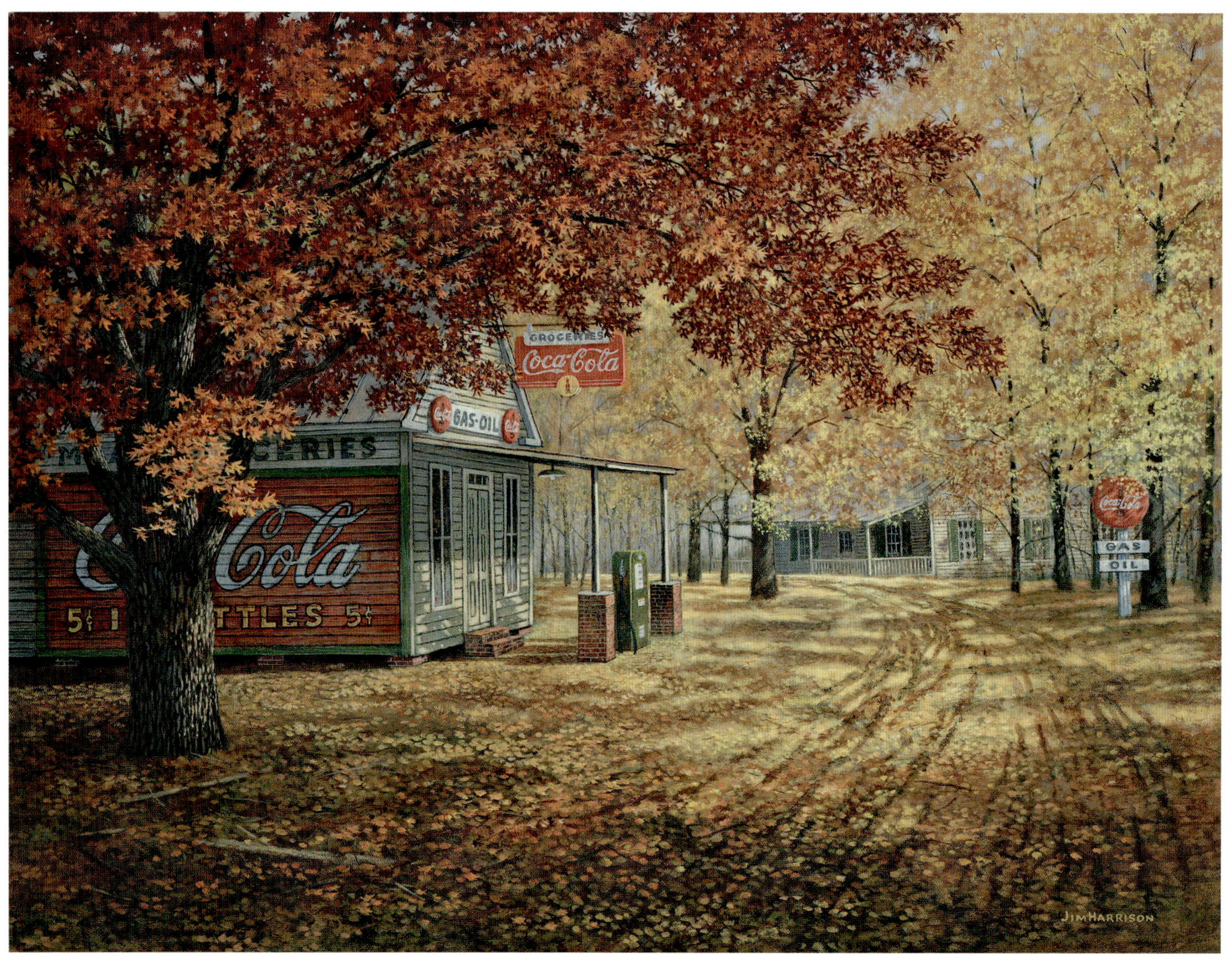


*September 2000*

ACRYLIC ON CANVAS, 22 × 28 INCHES, 1999

We didn't put up the tack on signs. Usually the delivery truck carried those, and the truck's driver nailed them on the building in a good space.

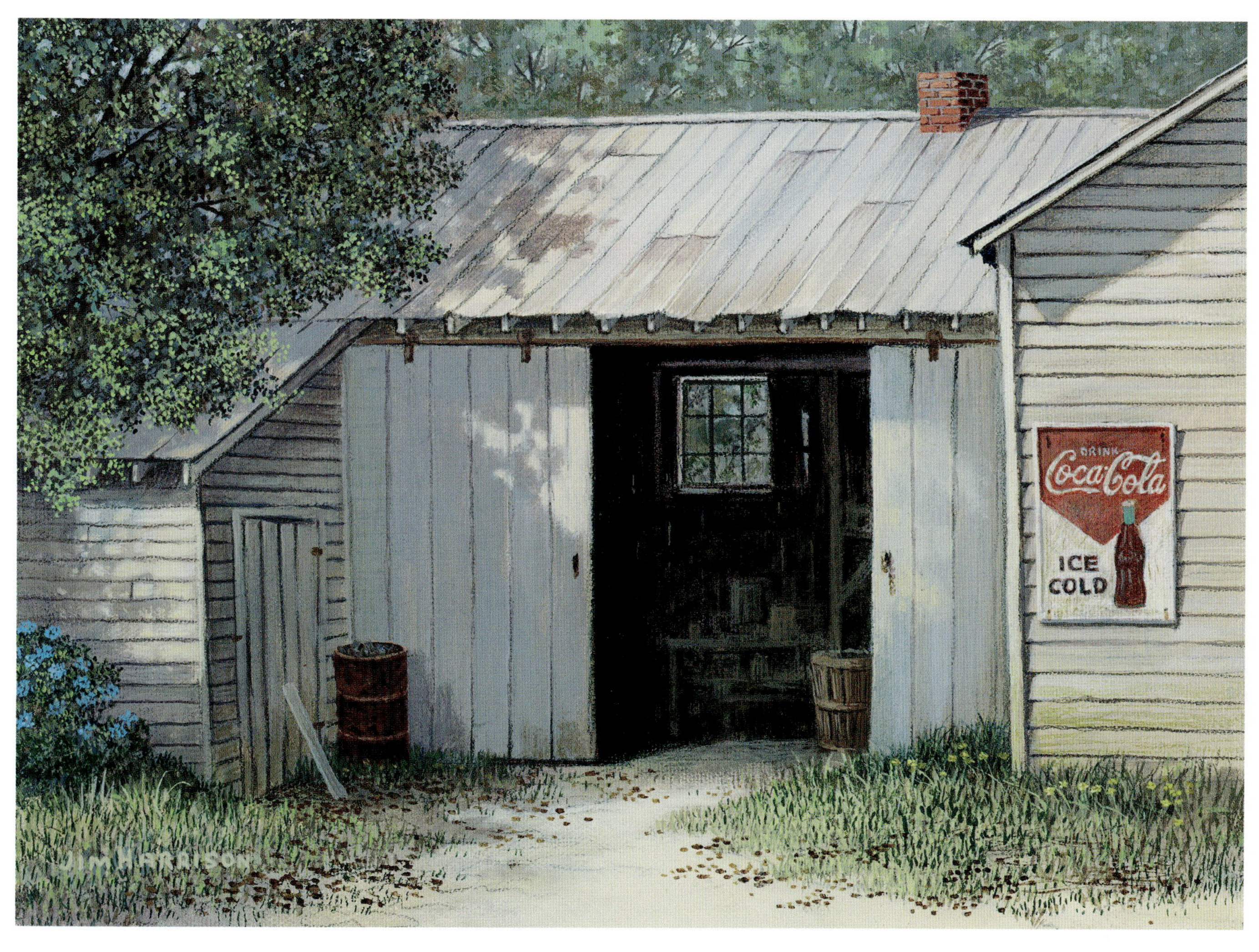


*September 2003*

ACRYLIC ON CANVAS, 9 × 12 INCHES, 1999

## *Coke Barn in Fall*

ACRYLIC ON CANVAS, 12 × 16 INCHES, 2012

Frequently, while working on one of the large outdoor bulletins, we would encounter other sign-painting crews traveling the country, maintaining the signs for national advertising concerns. The crews shared a common bond. And when lunch time would come, we would sit under the same tree and share tales of an era that was fast coming to an end. Often the conversation would run to the technical aspects of sign painting. We might be painting a Coca-Cola sign with a red background and white letters. Someone might say, "Well, do you know that in 1920 Coca-Cola would put a black border and a black shade on that Spencerian script that they use for their trademark?" And maybe they would argue about it or question one another about it. The conversations would run the gamut of the old-time sign painter's art and perhaps result in one of the men drawing a layout on the ground or on the paper bag. Every time he would do that, I would get that piece of paper and I'd keep it. Or if it was a drawing on the ground, I'd copy it. I kept all of those things showing the various ways signs were painted, so I had a wealth of information that I gathered during those lunch times while working for Mr. Cornforth.

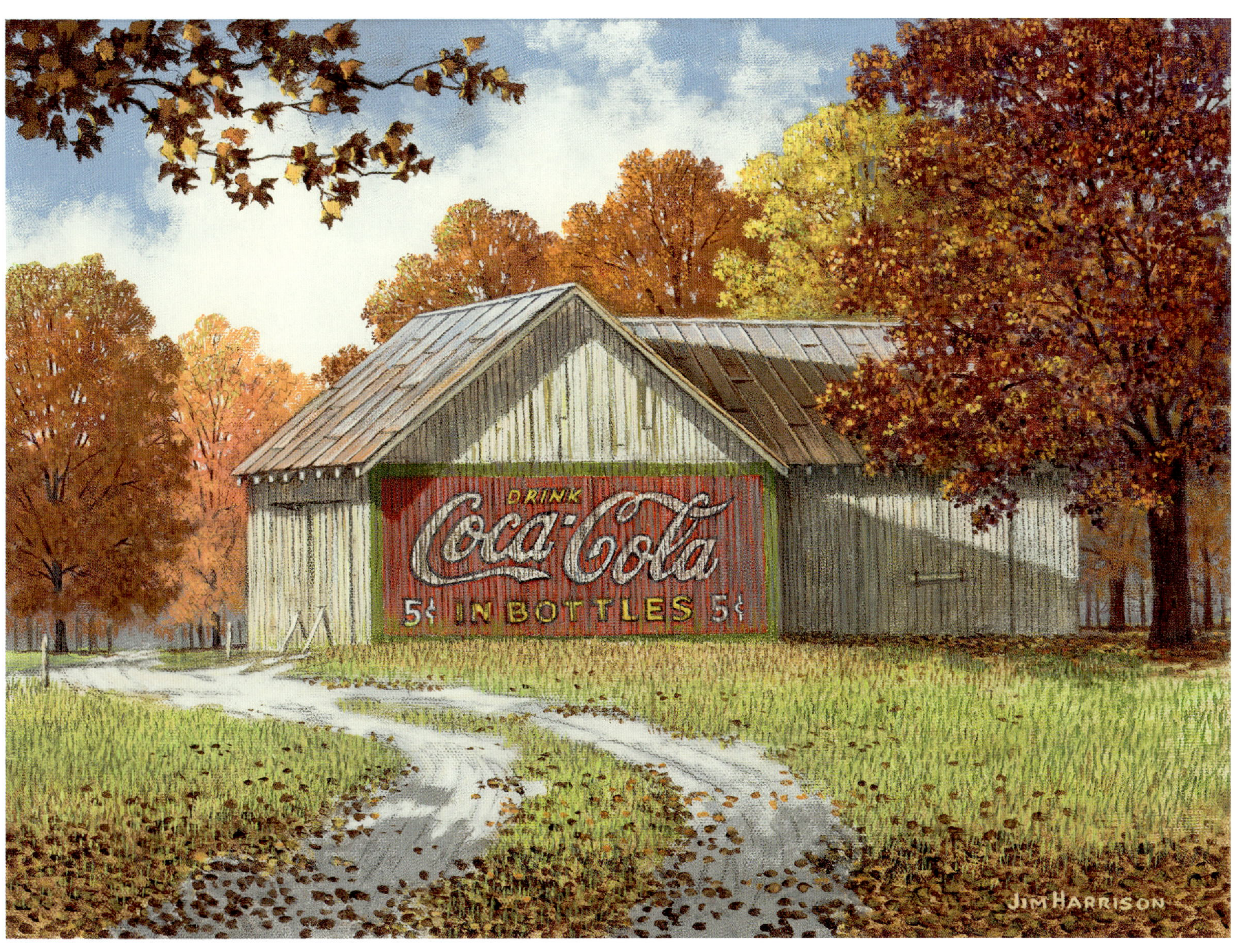
DRINK
Coca-Cola
5¢ IN BOTTLES 5¢
JIM HARRISON

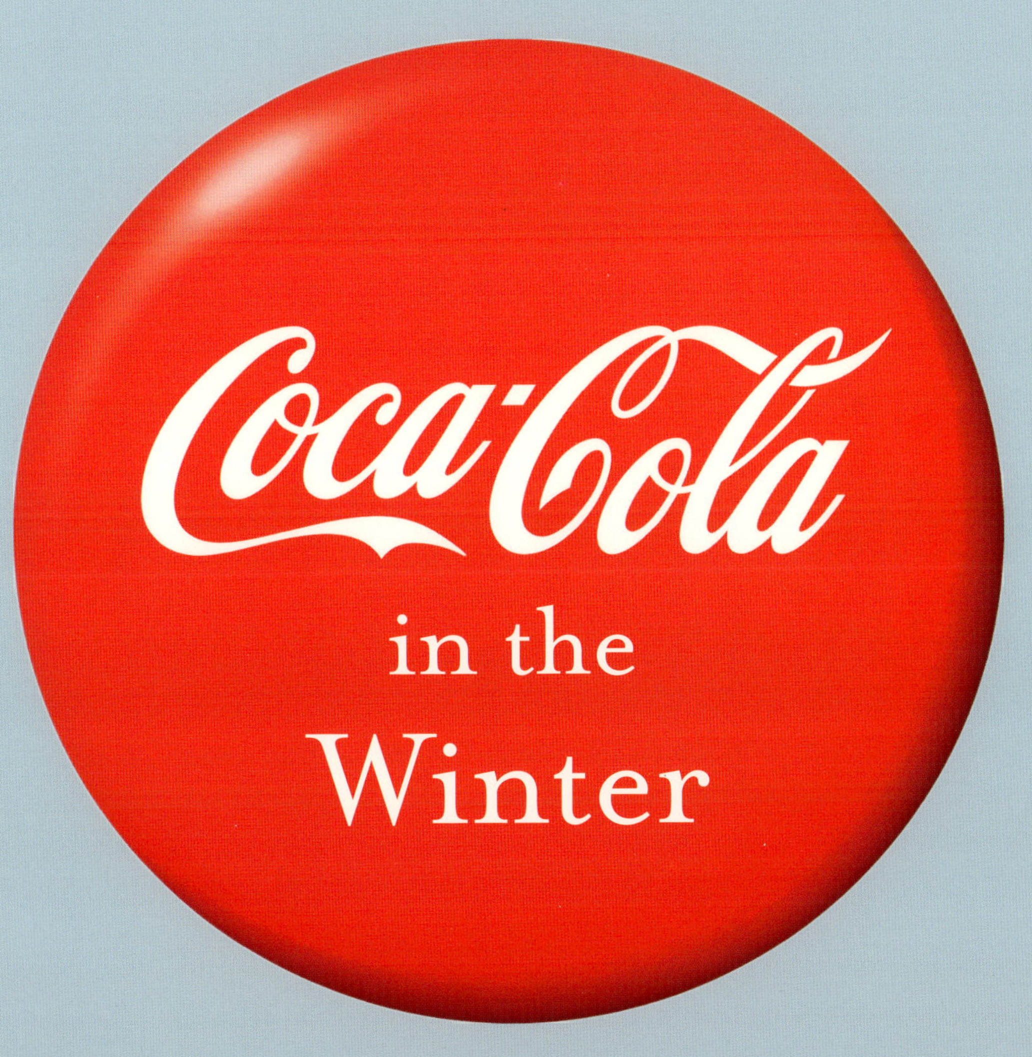
Coca-Cola
in the
Winter

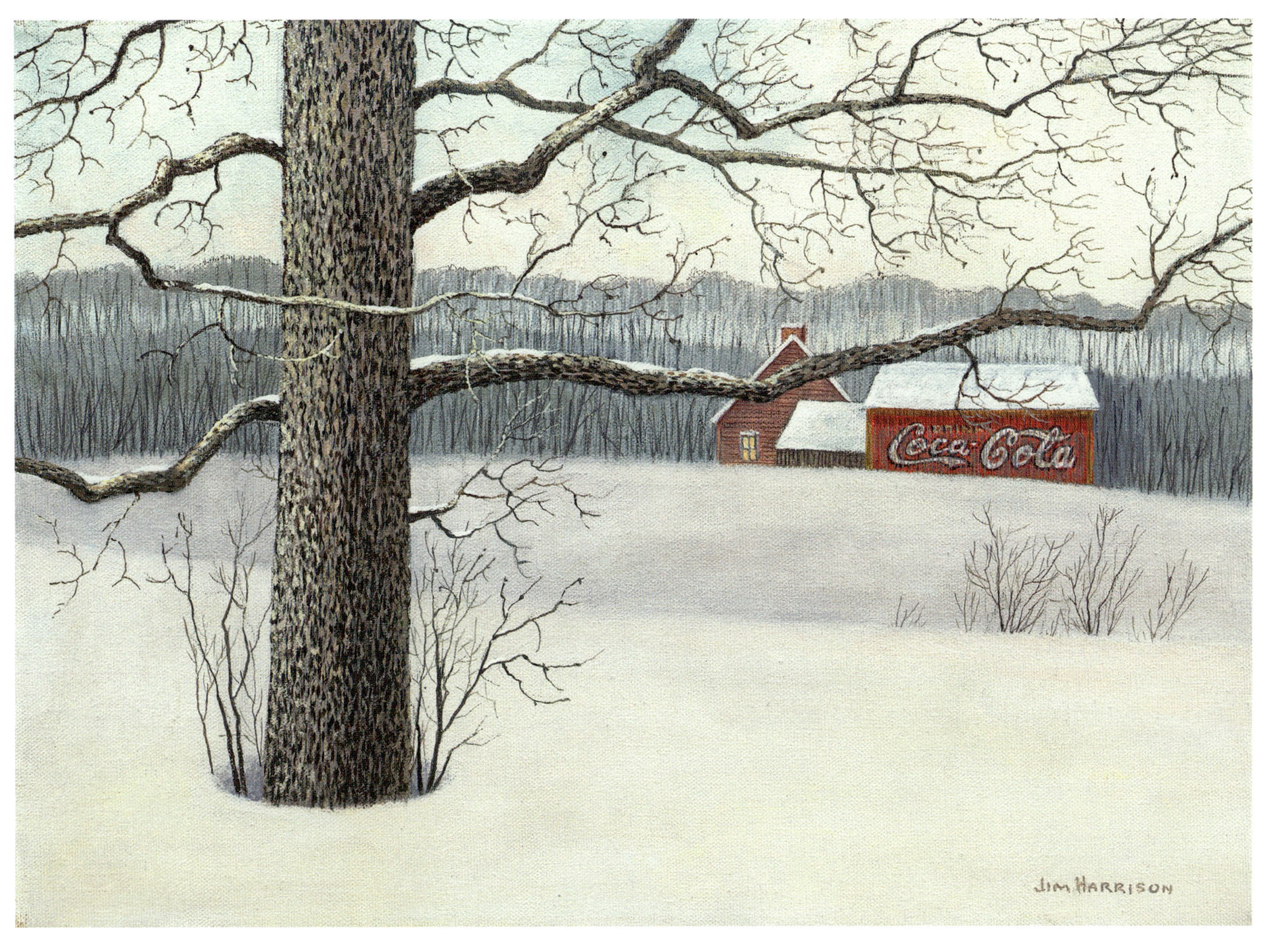


*Coca-Cola Winter Snow*

ACRYLIC ON CANVAS, 12 × 16 INCHES, 2001

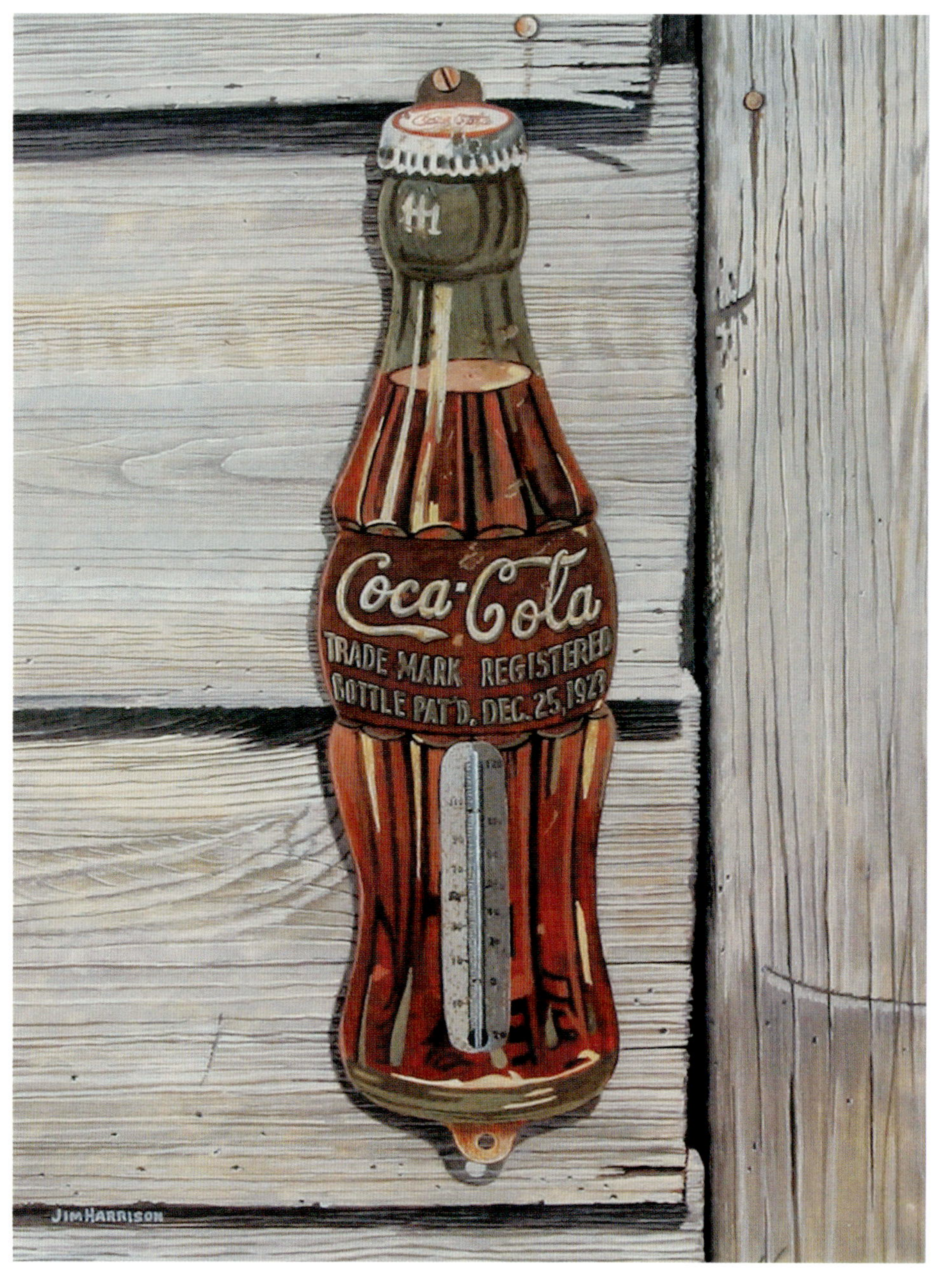


*Coca-Cola Christmas Thermometer*

WATERCOLOR ON ILLUSTRATION BOARD, 7 × 9.5 INCHES, 1978

"The Coca-Cola Christmas Thermometer" was so named because the bottle depicted was patented on Christmas Day.

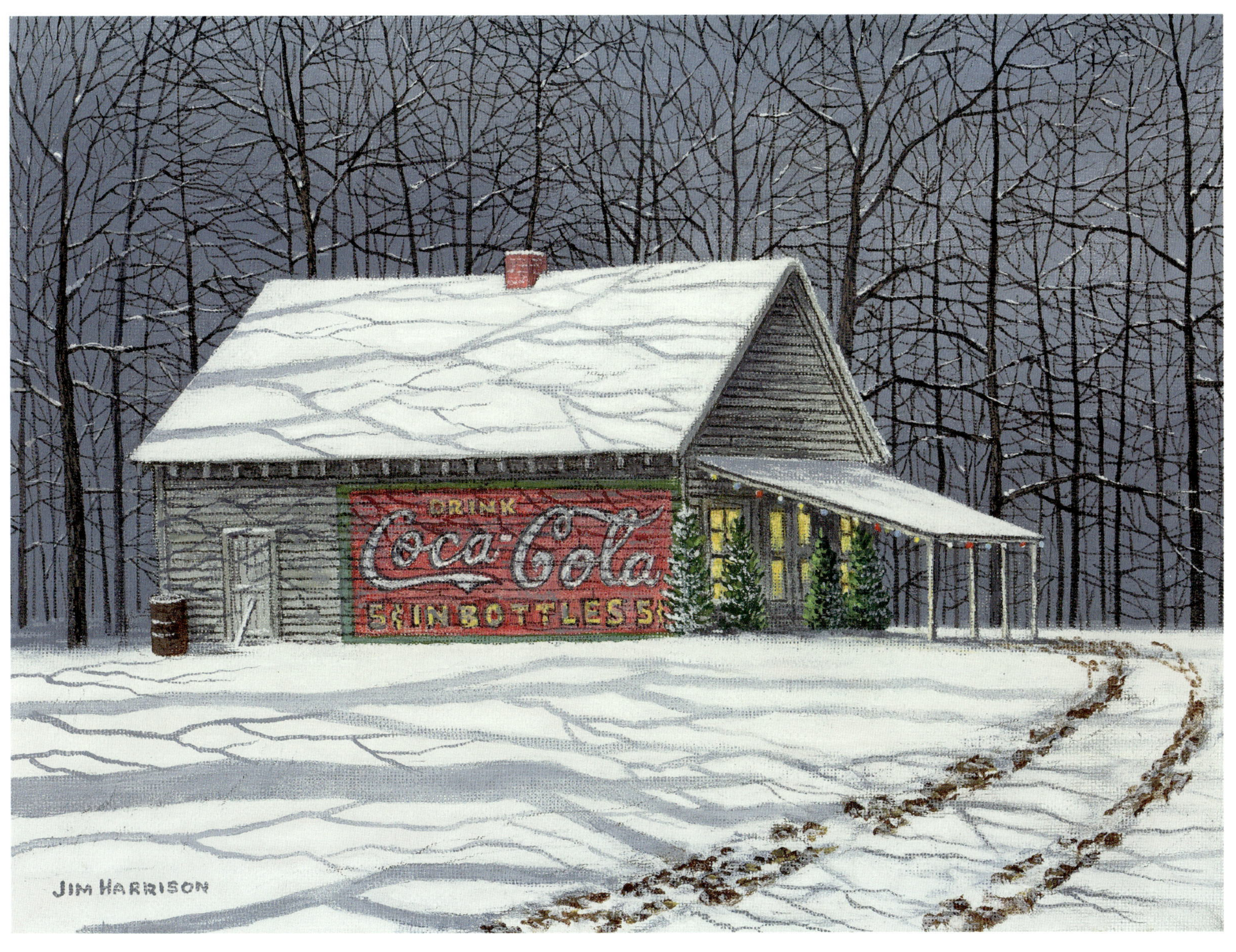


*Christmas Store*

ACRYLIC ON CANVAS, 9 × 12 INCHES, 2008

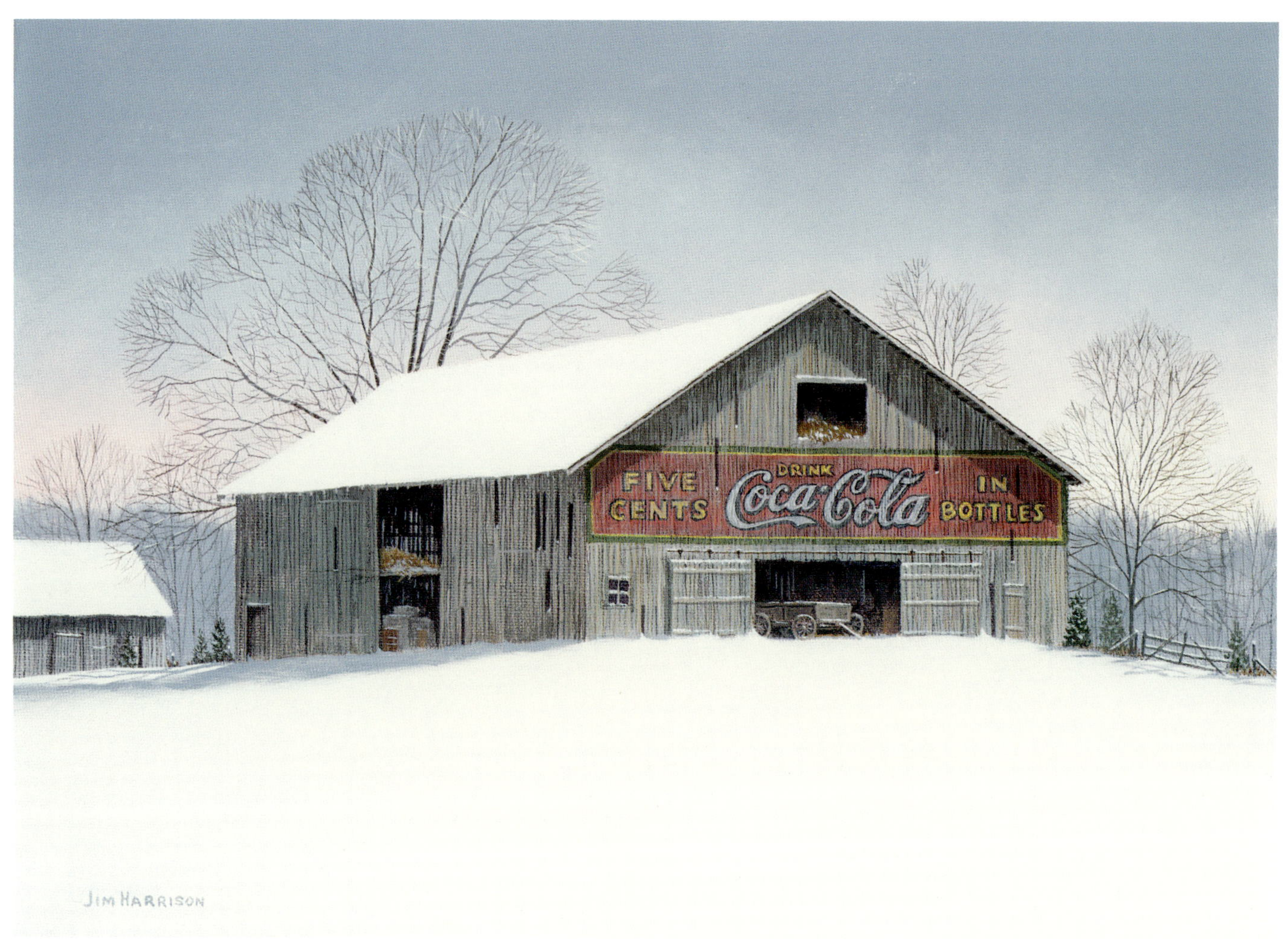


*Coca-Cola in Bottles*

ACRYLIC ON CANVAS, 12 × 16 INCHES, 2002

I sincerely try to put meaning into my work in hopes it has some historical value. With my paintbrush and pen, I sometimes feel like I'm just one step in front of the wrecking ball. For more than half a century, I have had a love affair with old buildings, old things, and old ways. Preserving them in at least some small way is important to me.

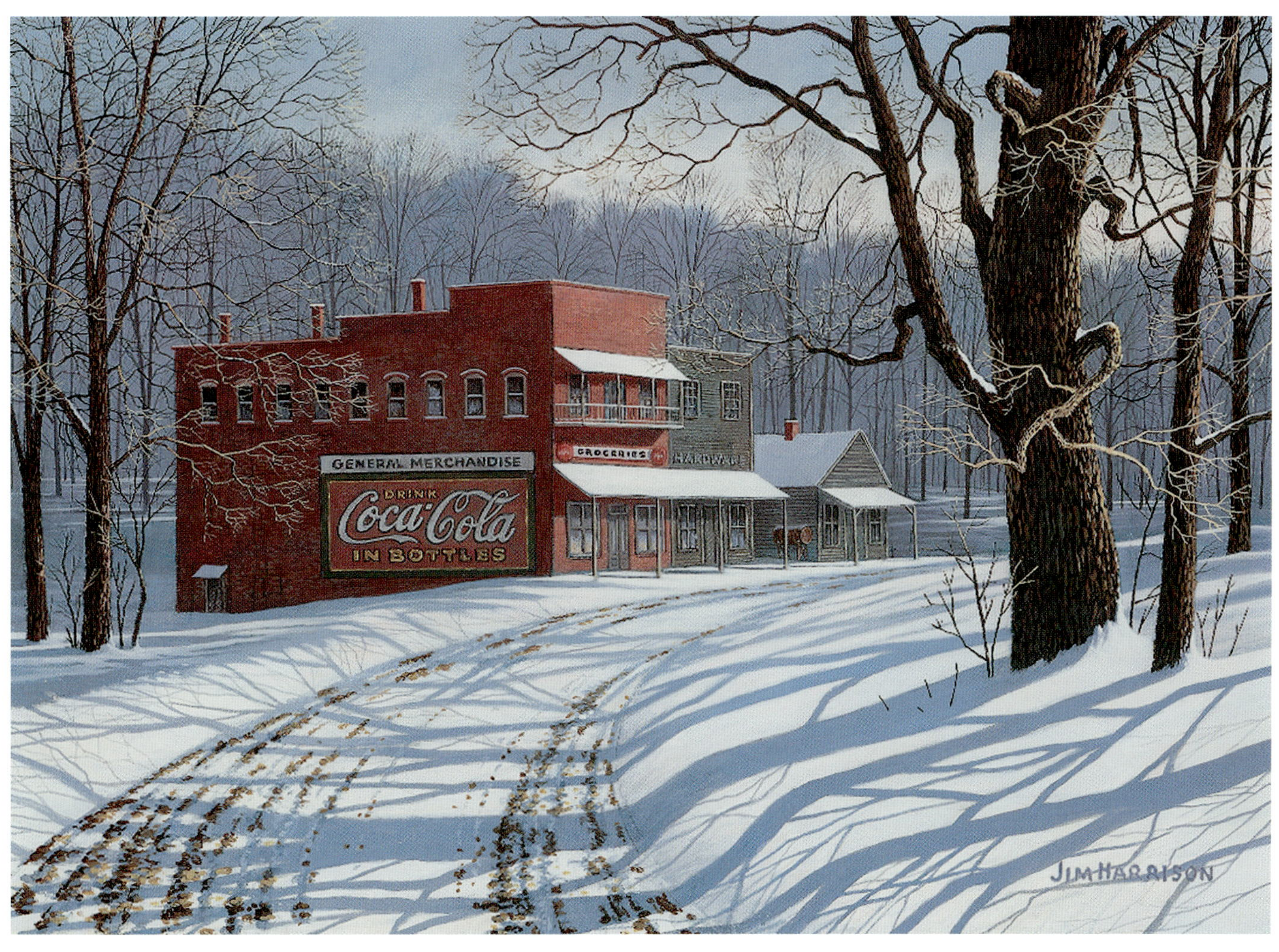


*Coca-Cola in Snow*

ACRYLIC ON MASONITE, 12 × 16 INCHES, 1996

Coca-Cola. Their ads show the ice-cold drink as enjoyable even in the snow. And it is.

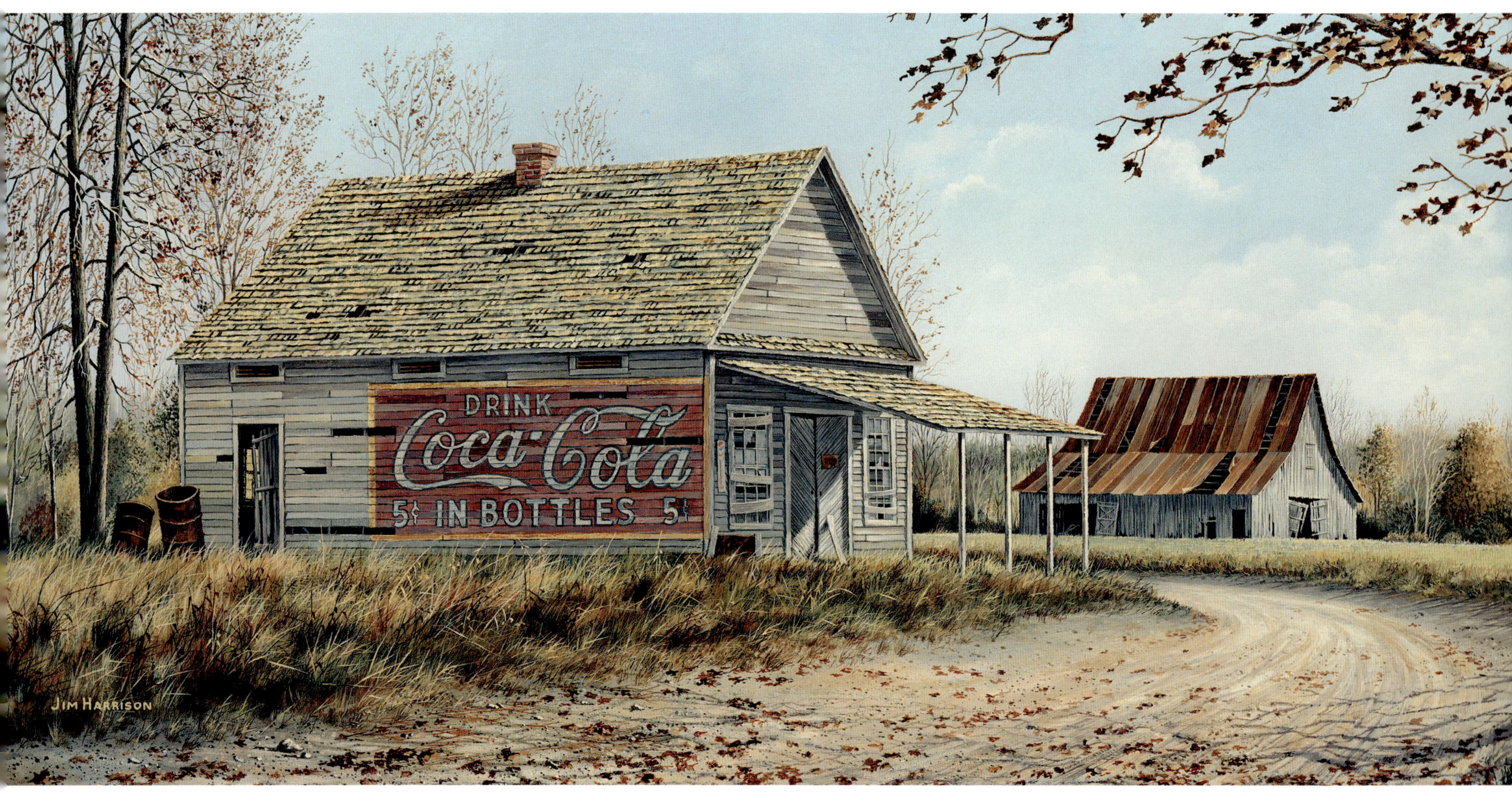


*Disappearing America*

acrylic on Masonite, 15 × 30 inches, 1973

Disappearing America was our first limited-edition fine-art Coca-Cola print on the market. It sold out immediately on release and increased in value of $3,800 at one point on the secondary market.

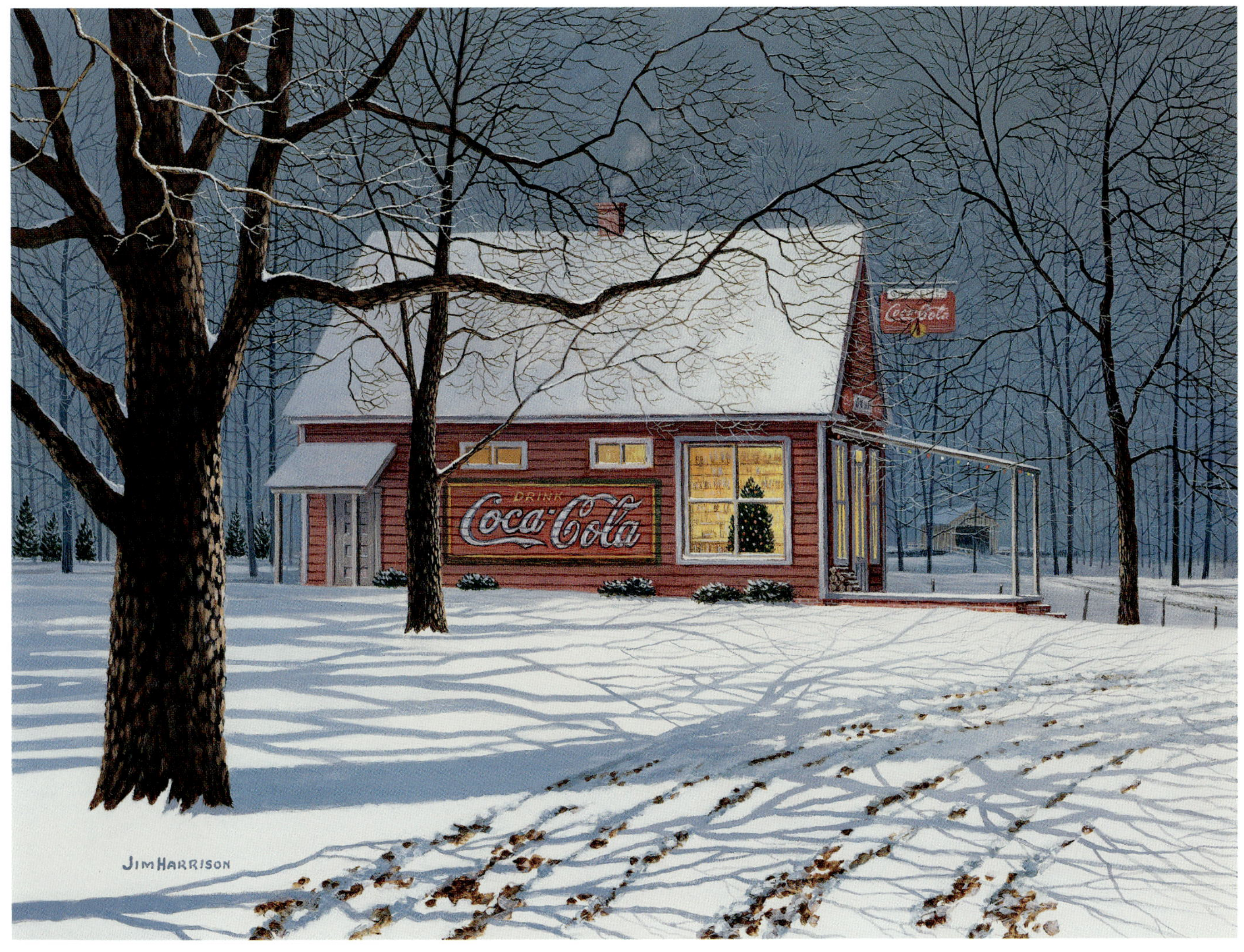


*Christmas Coca-Cola*

ACRYLIC ON ILLUSTRATION BOARD, 13 × 17 INCHES, 2001

The happy memories of carefree childhood days do indeed become the treasured mental keepsakes of a lifetime, and nothing warms our hearts more than a look backward.

## *Coca-Cola Bridge in Winter*

ACRYLIC ON MASONITE, 12 × 18 INCHES, 1996

Outdoor advertising can trace its lineage back to the earliest civilizations. Thousands of years ago, the Egyptians employed tall stone obelisks to publicize laws and treaties. While modes of advertising have changed over the centuries, outdoor advertising is still a relevant form of communication today. In the beginning, American roadside advertising was generally local. Merchants painted signs or glued posters on walls and fences to notify passersby that establishments up the road sold horse blankets, rheumatism pills, and other useful items. By 1870 nearly 300 small sign-painting and bill-posting companies were in operation. From these early beginnings, the modern billboard was born.

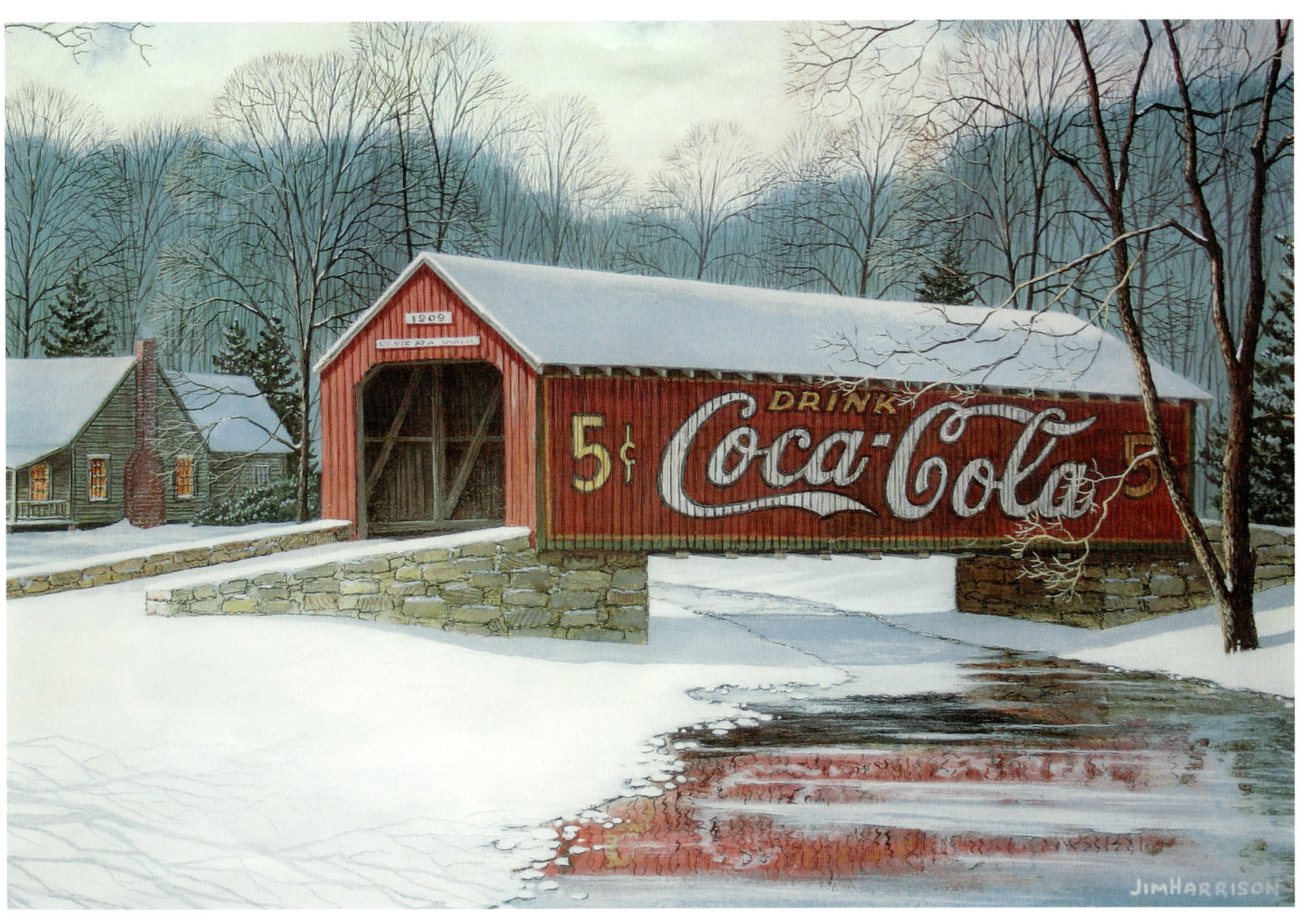
1809
DRINK
5¢
Coca-Cola
JIMHARRISON

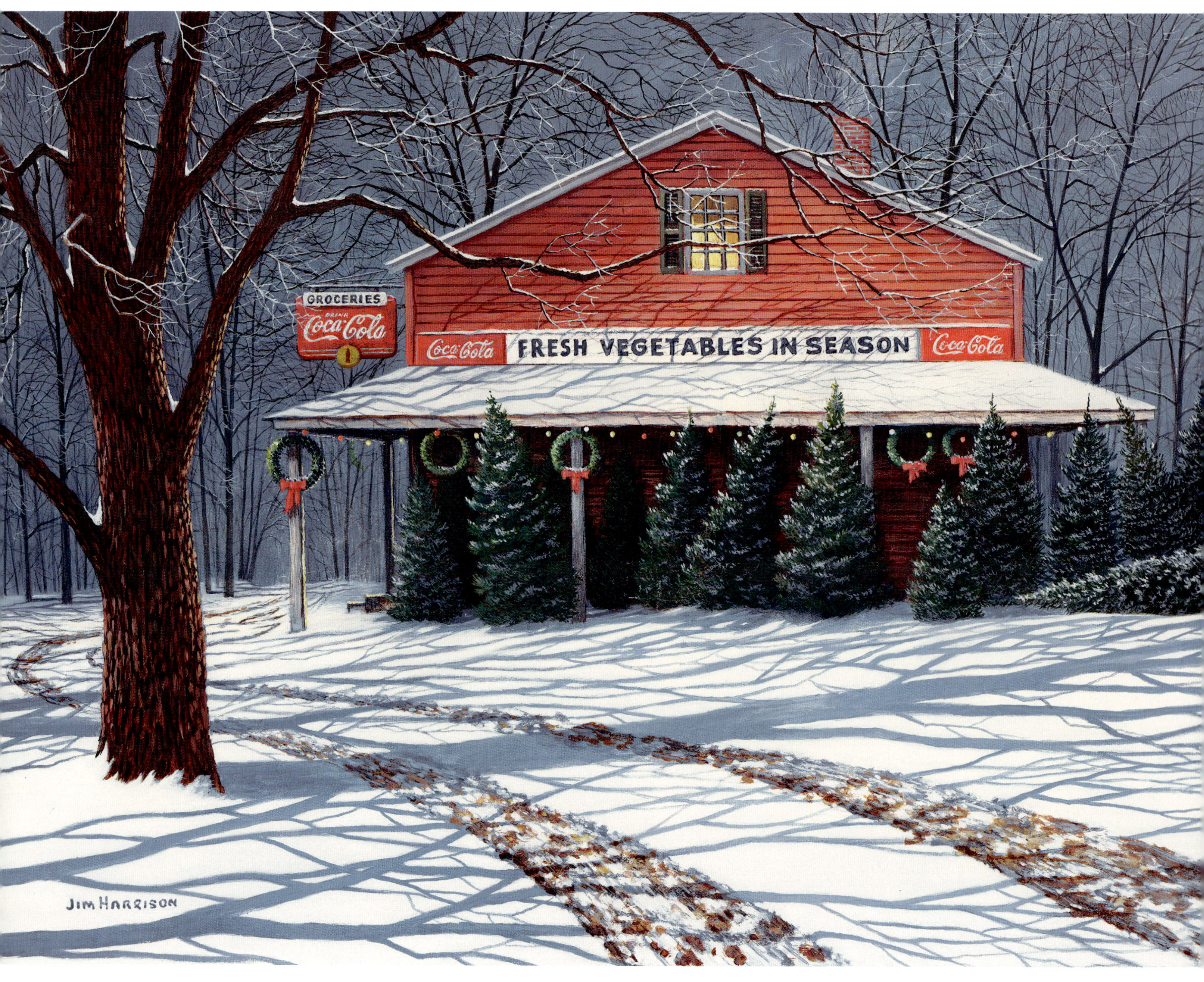
GROCERIES
Coca-Cola
Coca-Cola
FRESH VEGETABLES IN SEASON
Coca-Cola
JIM HARRISON

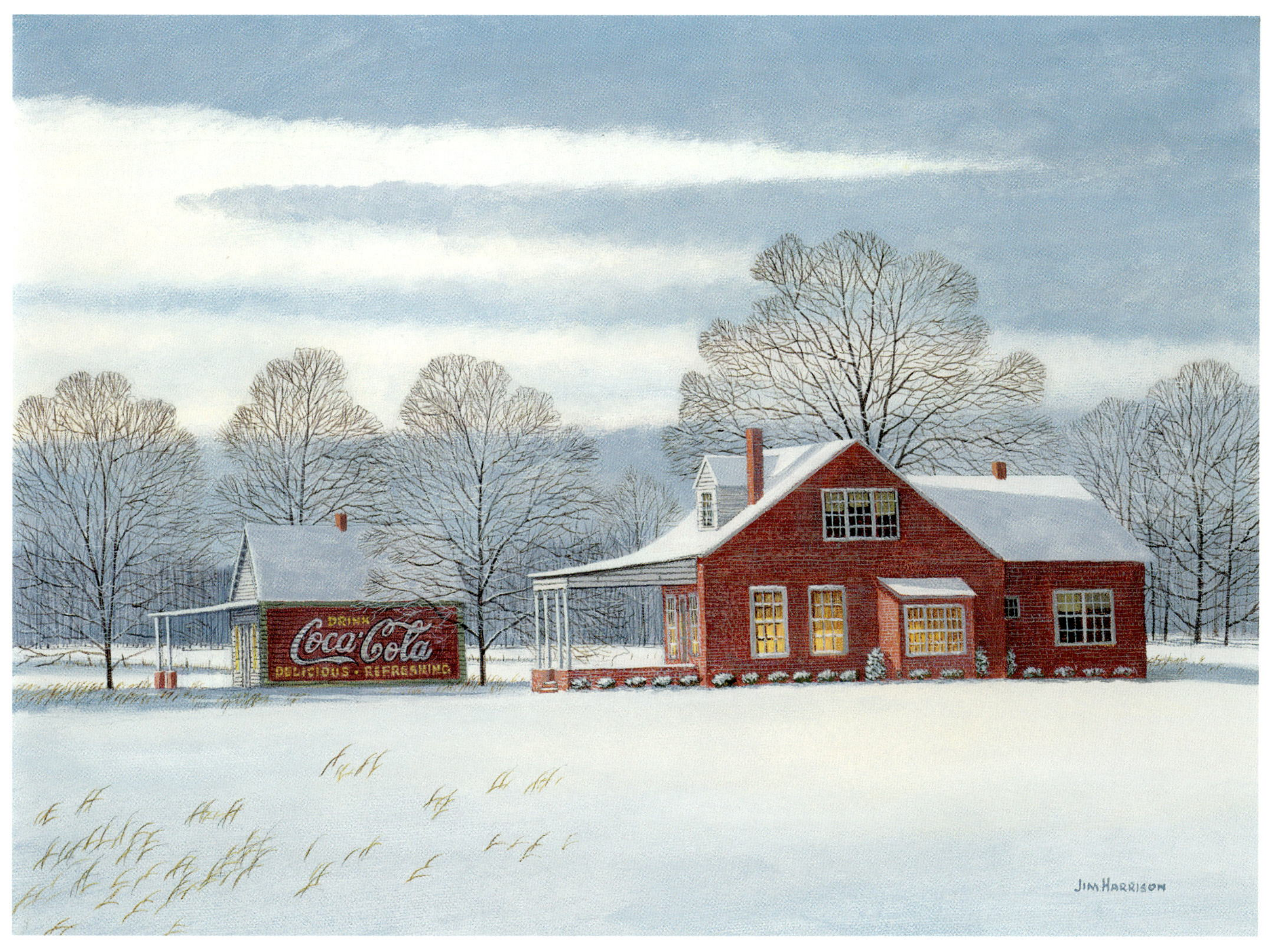


*Coca-Cola February*

ACRYLIC ON CANVAS, 12 × 16 INCHES, 1999

I love the snow. The falling of snow seems to bring with it a coziness of family and friends gathering around a warm fire.

FACING *Coca-Cola Christmas Trees*

ACRYLIC ON ILLUSTRATION BOARD, 13 × 17 INCHES, 2000

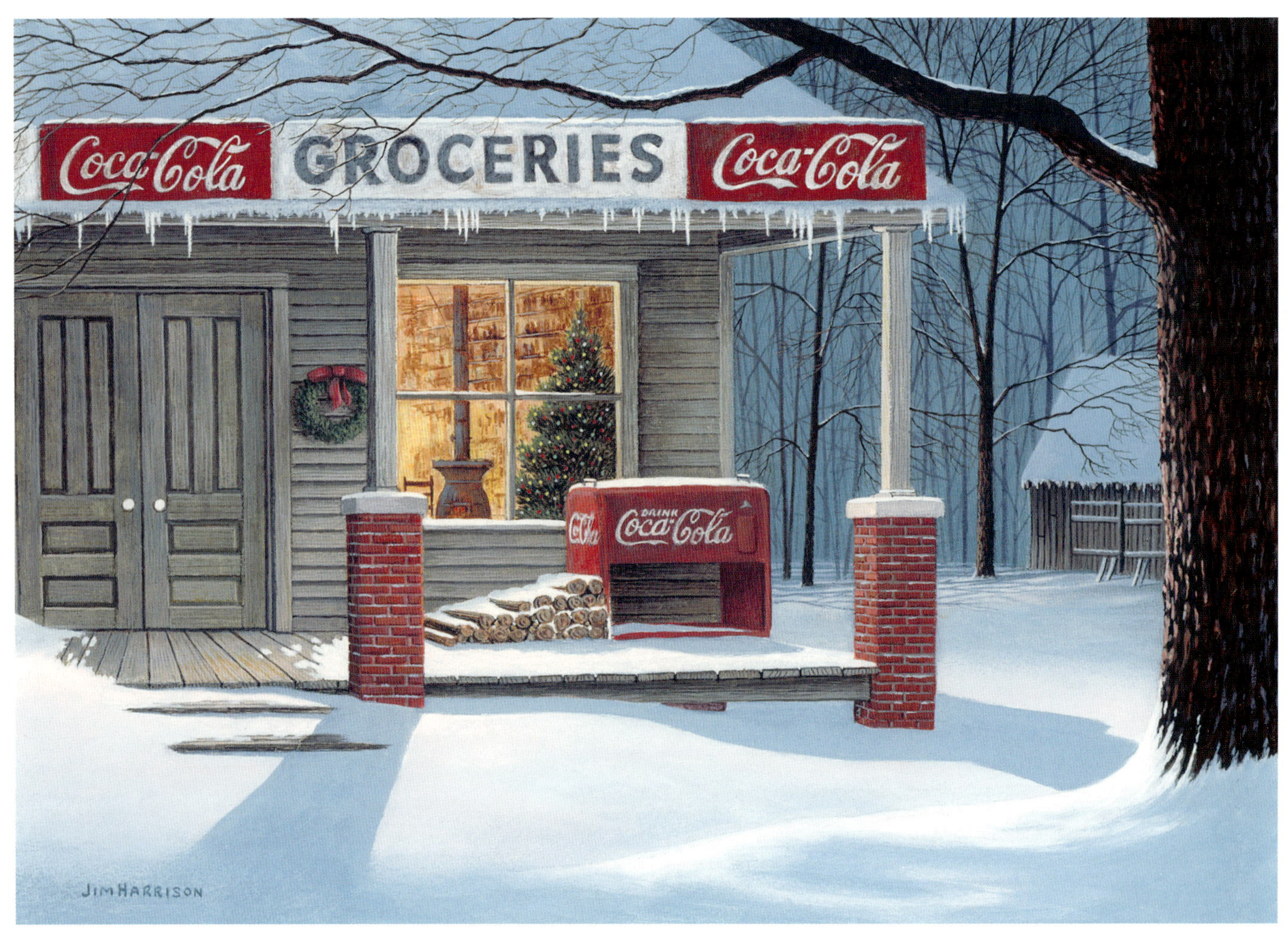


*Coca-Cola Groceries*

ACRYLIC ON CANVAS, 12 × 16 INCHES, 1996

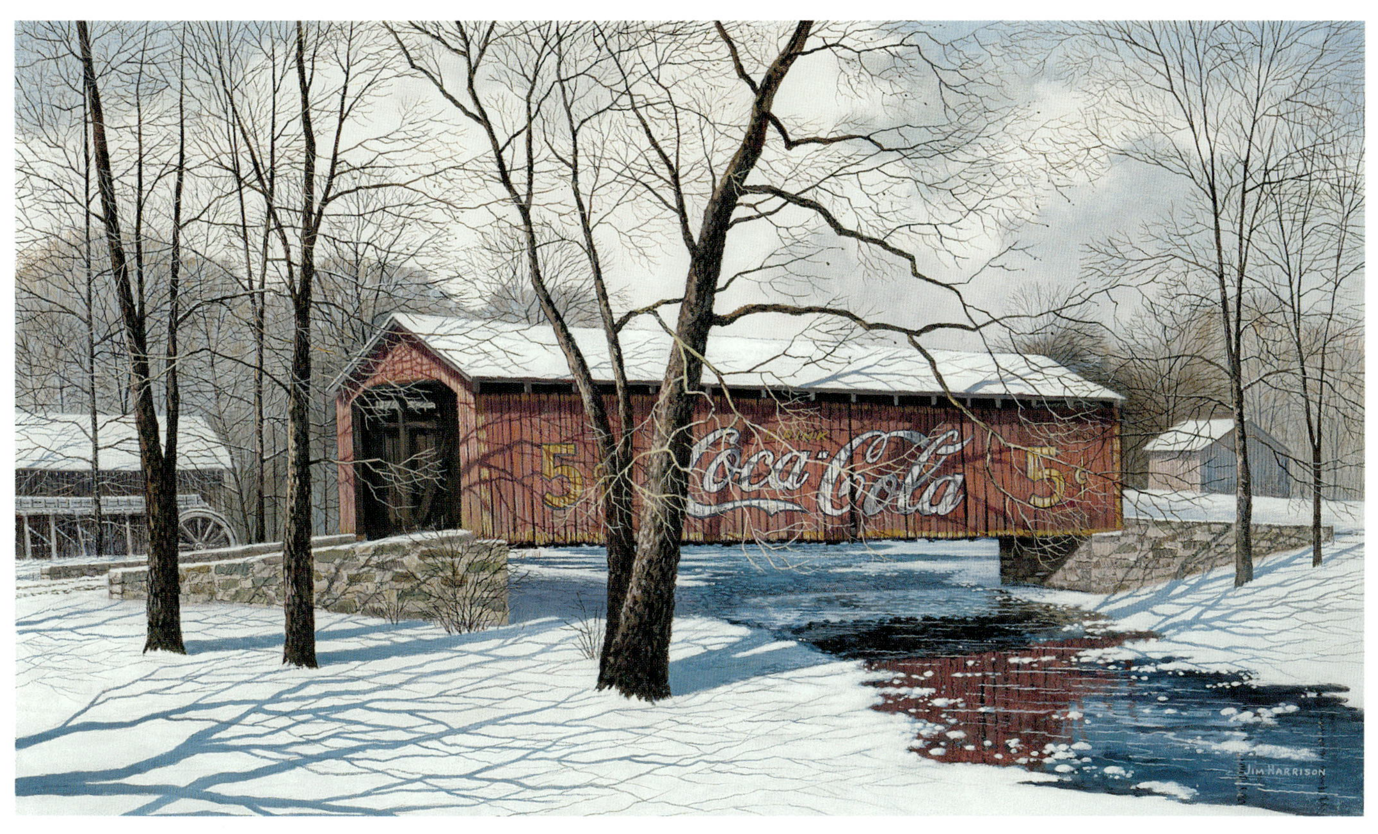


*Coca-Cola Snow-Covered Bridge*

ACRYLIC ON CANVAS, 20 × 30 INCHES, 2004

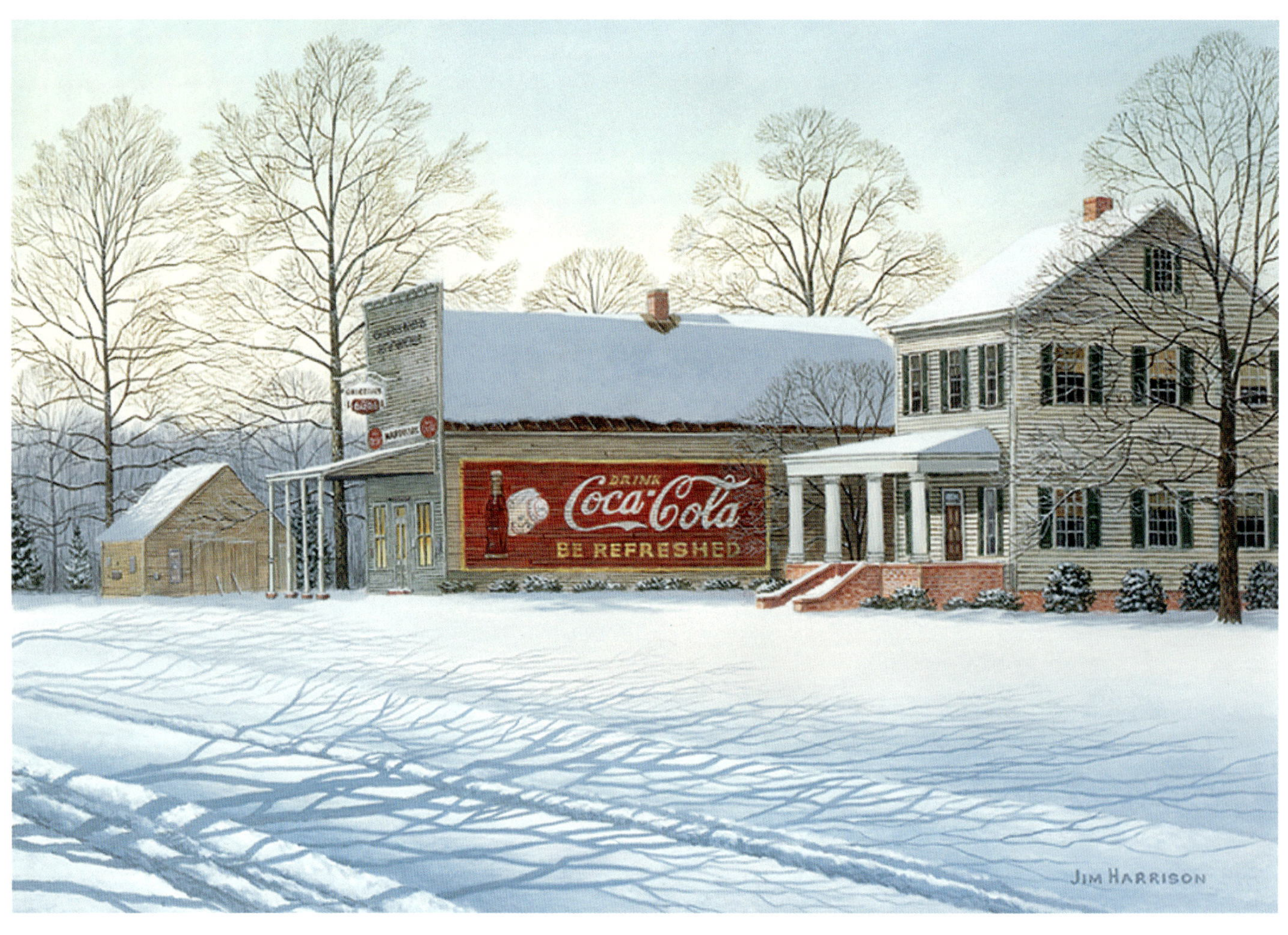


*Coca-Cola Store in Snow*

ACRYLIC ON ILLUSTRATION BOARD, 13 × 17.5 INCHES, 1997

A solid white covering of freshly fallen snow gives a clean pristine look to the landscape that is most appealing to me as fan and artist. I enjoy painting it. Problem is I don't see it often enough. Every few years we get a good snow, and I'm out in it with my camera, gathering reference photos.

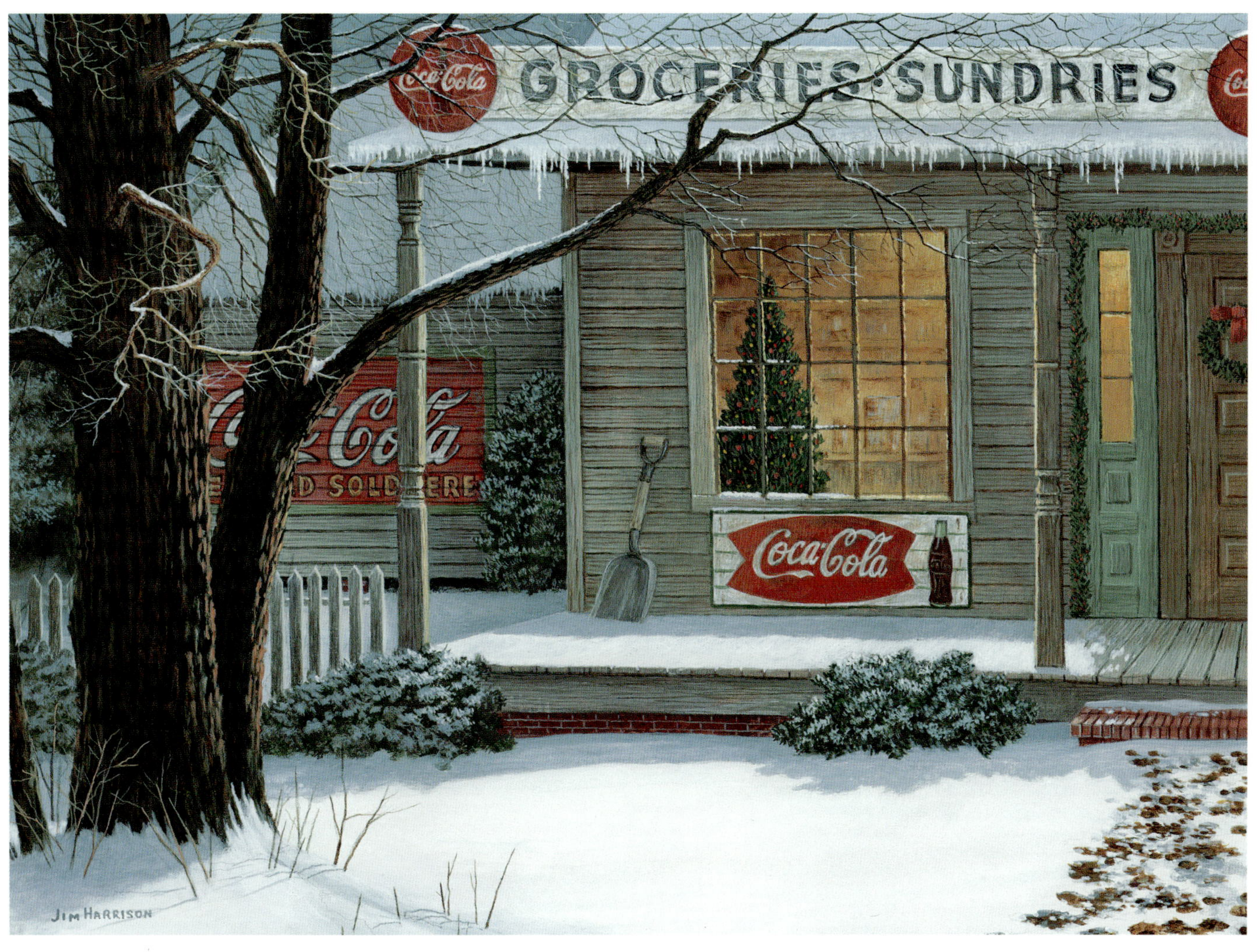


*December 2000*

ACRYLIC ON ILLUSTRATION BOARD, 11 × 15 INCHES, 1999

I am so glad that I live in an area where we experience the four different seasons. Quarterly we begin the anticipation of the next season and the changes that will come with it. We must adjust our wardrobe, rearrange our yard furniture, and adjust things in our homes. Businesses begin presenting the next seasonal items well in advance. The regular changes are good for our spirits.

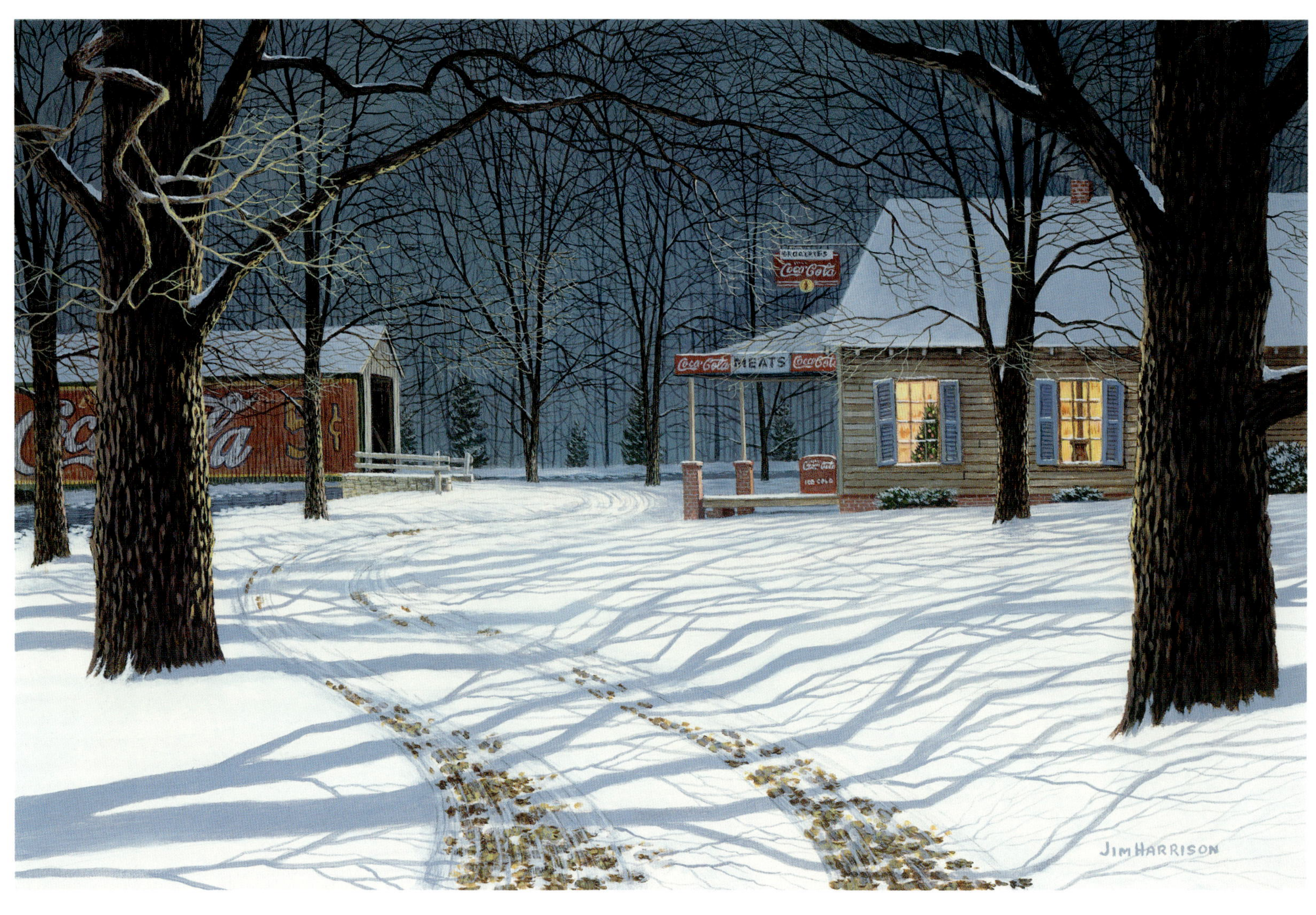


*December 1999*

ACRYLIC ON ILLUSTRATION BOARD, 11 × 15 INCHES, 1998

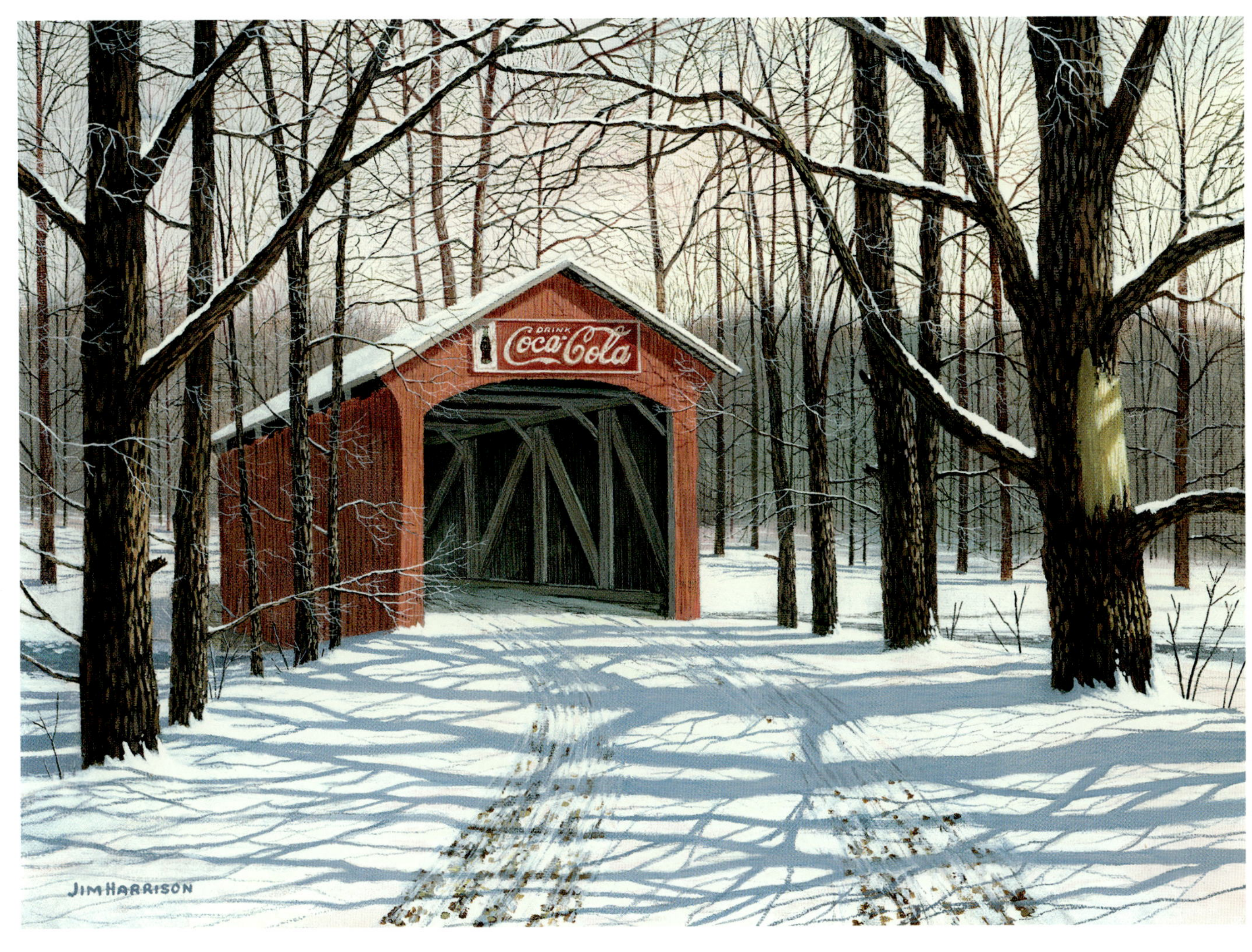


*February 1998*

ACRYLIC ON CANVAS, 12 × 16 INCHES, 1997

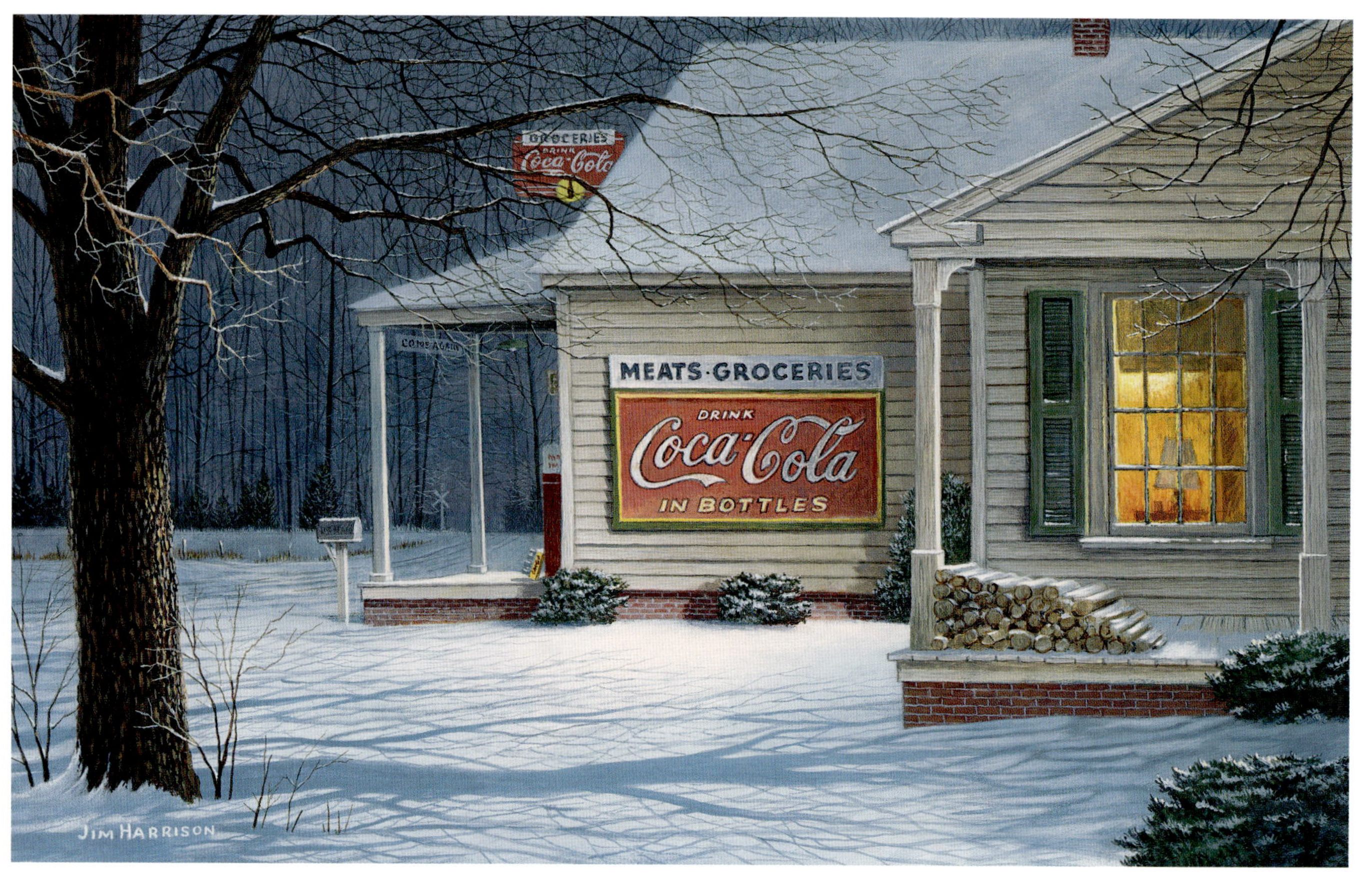


*January 2000*

ACRYLIC ON ILLUSTRATION BOARD, 10.5 × 17 INCHES, 1999

FACING *January 2001*

ACRYLIC ON ILLUSTRATION BOARD, 11 × 16 INCHES, 1998

I now feel that I have come full circle. Working with Coca-Cola to capture the trademark along with images of the past is a natural partnership. I am as excited about this work as I was many years ago when I crawled up on that first Coca-Cola wall with Mr. Cornforth. Since entering into a licensee relationship with Coca-Cola in 1995, I have continued developing limited-edition prints using the trademark. I have also begun developing other products with the trademark, including canvas transfers, trays, sun catchers, and calendars.

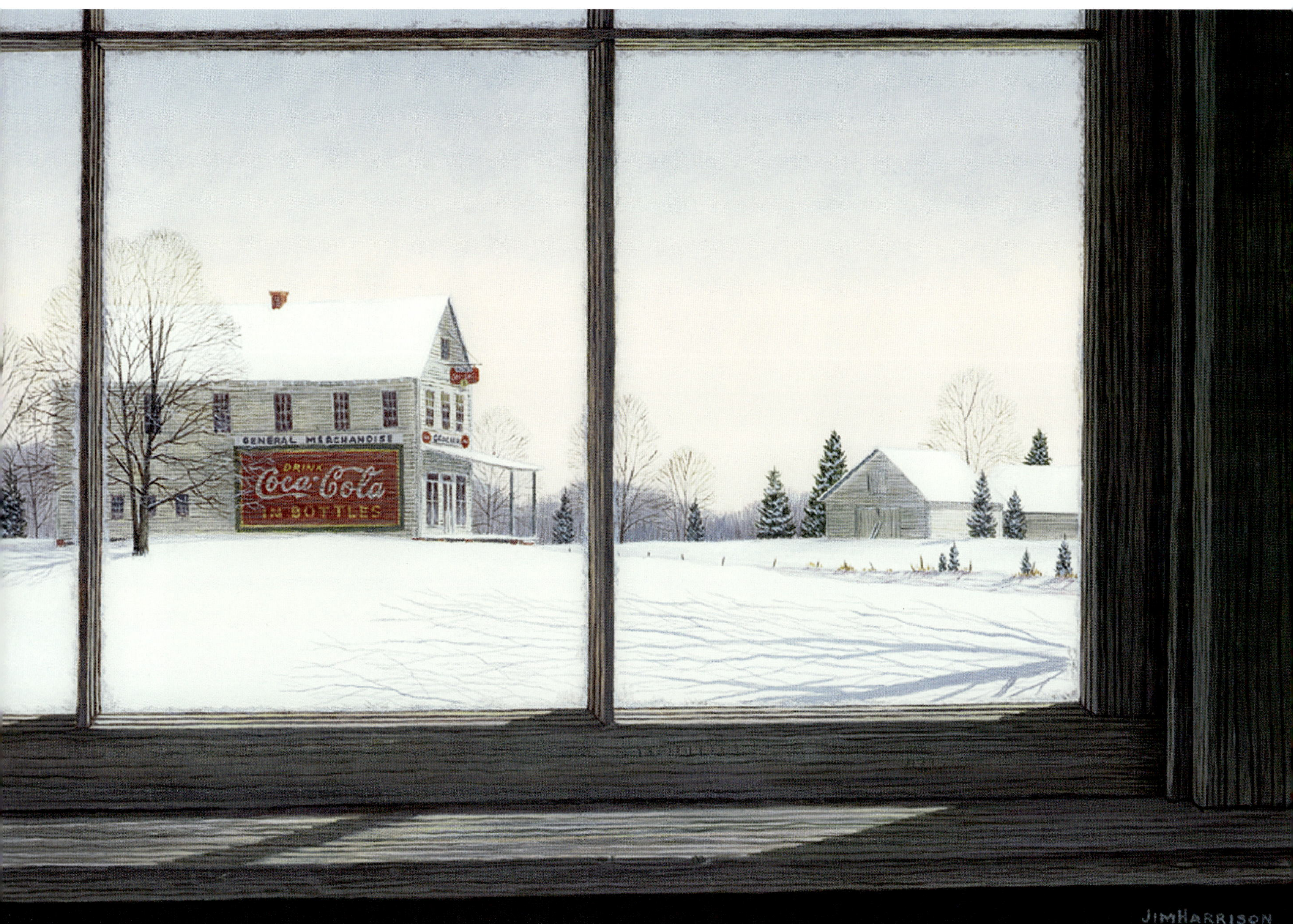
GENERAL MERCHANDISE
DRINK
Coca-Cola
IN BOTTLES
JIMHARRISON

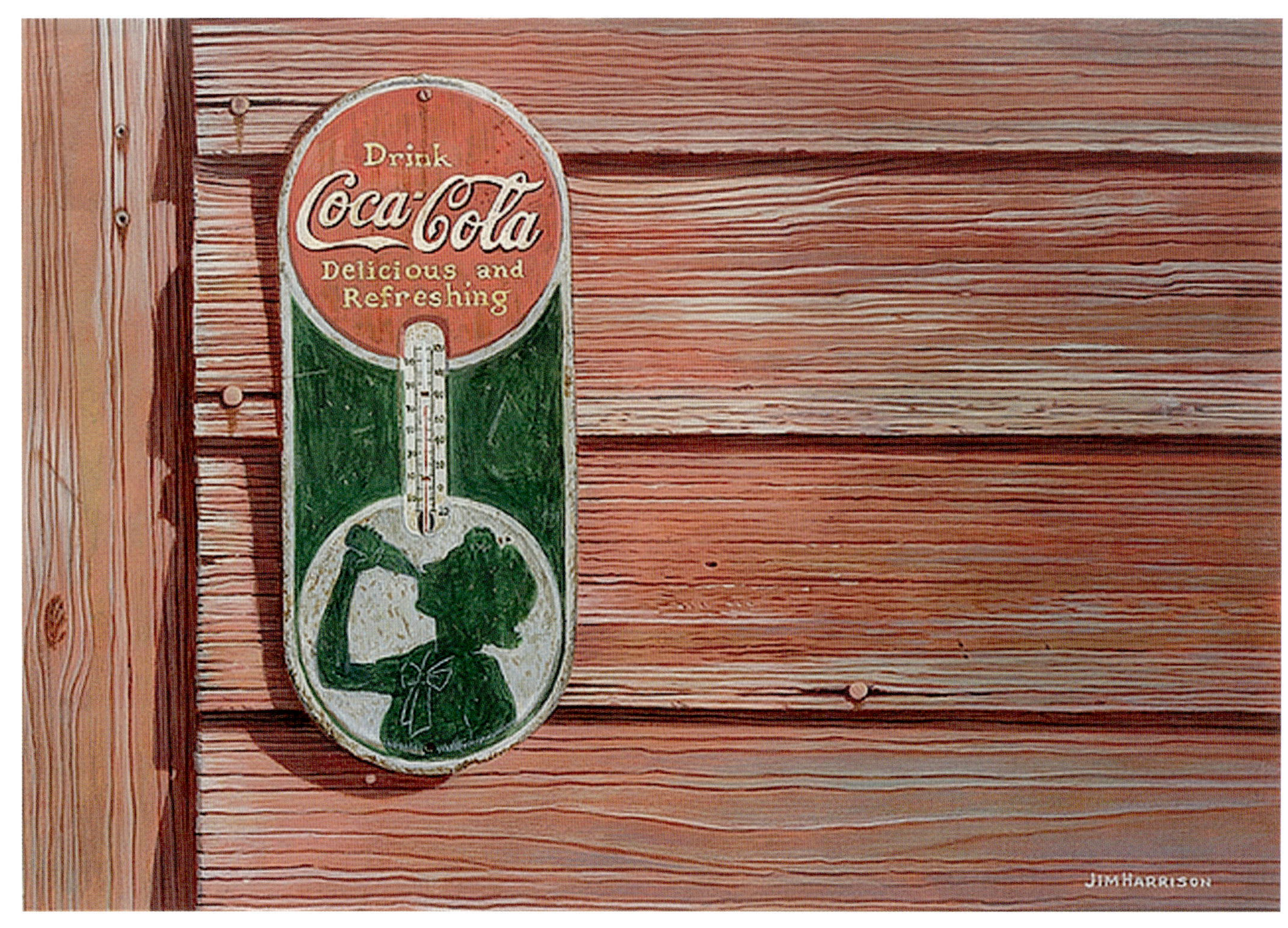


*1939 Coca-Cola Thermometer*

ACRYLIC ON ILLUSTRATION BOARD, 12 × 16 INCHES, 1998

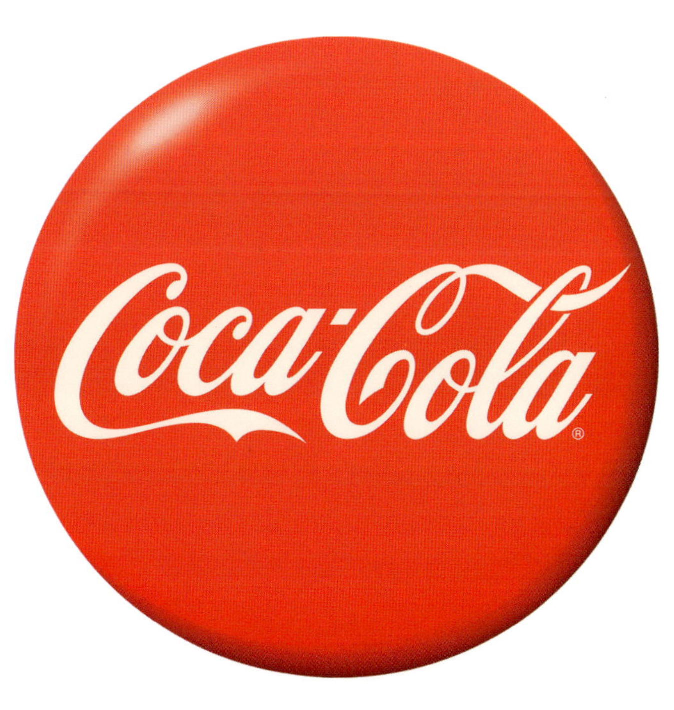
Coca-Cola®

# INDEX OF THE PAINTINGS